CW01249407

RE-THINKING RETAIL
IN THE DIGITAL ERA

THE ELIX-IRR PARTNERSHIP

THE ELIX-IRR PARTNERSHIP is a firm of entrepreneurs who share a common purpose of impartially serving clients to make them more successful by aligning our goals and challenging conventional market norms.

We are creating the firm that we want – a global team that is easy to engage with, that combines the very best of business and consulting leaders and develops talent to achieve success.

We believe that great client relationships and mutual support and respect for one another will lead to the highest quality services and greater success for our clients, our firm and our people.

As partners we are committed to clear thinking and honest dialogue and believe that our newest recruit will one day lead our firm.

www.elix-irr.com

RE-THINKING RETAIL
IN THE DIGITAL ERA

WRITTEN AND EDITED BY ELIX-IRR

LID

LONDON   NEW YORK   SHANGHAI
MADRID   BARCELONA   BOGOTA
MEXICO CITY   MONTERREY   BUENOS AIRES

Published by
LID Publishing Ltd
The Loft, 19a Floral Street
Covent Garden
London WC2E 9DS
United Kingdom
info@lidpublishing.com
www.lidpublishing.com

A member of:
BPR
Business Publishers Roundtable
www.businesspublishersroundtable.com

All rights reserved. Without limiting the rights under copyright reserved, no part of this publication may be reproduced, stored or introduced into a retrieval system, or transmitted, in any form or by any means (electronic, mechanical, photocopying, recording or otherwise) without the prior written permission of both the copyright owners and the publisher of this book.

© Elix-IRR
© LID Publishing Ltd, 2014

ISBN: 978-1-907794-62-9

Cover and page design: Laura Hawkins

CONTENTS

FOREWORD	6
1. RETAIL STRATEGY	8
1.1 Customers are transforming retail	11
1.2 Digital's underlying dynamics	20
1.3 Digital platforms	34
1.4 The rise of digital money	44
2. DRIVING EFFICIENCY & INSIGHT	50
2.1 The customer returns opportunity	53
2.2 Integrated business planning	60
2.3 Big data in retail	66
3. ORGANIZING FOR SUCCESS	74
3.1 Making business transformation a success	76
3.2 Organisational excellence through service management	84
3.3 Removing the "T" from your TOM	91
4. OUTSOURCING IN RETAIL	96
4.1 Outsourcing: delivering the expected benefits	99
4.2 The rise of "nearshoring"	113
4.3 Retail IT sourcing today	125
4.4 To RFP or not to RFP Using collaborative sourcing as a viable alternative	132
ELIX-IRR'S SENIOR TEAM	140
FIGURES	144
BIBLIOGRAPHY	146

FOREWORD

THERE IS LITTLE doubt that retailing around the world is experiencing some of the most interesting and challenging times in its history.

There are the global economic changes with low or no growth economies in the West, fast-growing markets in the East and new growth across Africa. Additionally, consumer markets are at the mercy of political shifts, whether through the rise of the middle classes or the search for greater democracy.

No shift is, however, more profound than the rise of the internet economy and the next wave of change largely attributable to the rise of digitally enabled consumers. One might have expected that the internet would by now have simply become business as usual for retailers whose adaptability to the changing consumer is second to none. However, the behavioural shift associated with the digital era is arguably so profound that it requires retailers not simply to act differently, but to think differently, and even to challenge the organisational and cultural structures on which they have been traditionally built.

In this collection of articles, Elix-IRR's retail professionals examine the fundamental changes brought about by the digital consumer and the related shifts in the sector. The articles discuss many of the challenges and opportunities on which our clients seek our advice. These are not only the fashionable issues of customer insight and multichannel shopping, but also the problems that arise through organisational change, the drive for supply chain efficiency and the transformation of IT from a back office cost centre to the enabling mechanism for all customer interaction and loyalty.

As a strategic advisory firm, Elix-IRR offers bespoke and differentiated advice on planning and executing these transformations, advice that is primarily focused on the creation of business value. Our team is composed of senior professionals from top-tier consulting and services firms, as well as experienced practitioners from industry. We provide inspiration and drive at every step of the transformation process, from defining business strategy, through operating model design and strategic sourcing, to the alignment of major change initiatives.

I hope you find that these articles provide some of the insightful, practical and pragmatic advice that we strive to deliver for our clients.

BRIAN KALMS,
ELIX-IRR RETAIL PARTNER,
brian.kalms@elix-irr.com

1. RETAIL STRATEGY

CHAPTER OVERVIEW

In this chapter, we discuss four key elements of the emerging retail landscape: customers, digital's underlying dynamics, digital platforms and the rise of digital payments.

1.1 CUSTOMERS ARE TRANSFORMING RETAIL

With the advent of digital channels and technology enabling constant consumer connectivity, retailers are faced with the challenge of keeping up with new innovations disrupting the market.

However, technology alone is not the driver behind the seismic shifts in today's customer engagement models. Customers are the real catalysts. Therefore, meeting customer expectations consistently across all physical and digital channels is a critical challenge for all retailers.

We explore how this new breed of digital-savvy, cost-conscious and impatient shoppers have shaped the multichannel retail landscape, and how retailers can respond.

1.2 DIGITAL'S UNDERLYING DYNAMICS

The term "digital" and its related trends are often reported upon and discussed in today's media; the explosion of social media, the rise of the smartphone, the promise of big data (and little data), the flexibility of the Cloud, the imperative of multichannel, the need for customer-centricity and the demise of high-street retailers such as HMV, Jessops and Blockbuster are very well publicized.

Digital technology, and innovative business models built around such technology, are topical and are significantly impacting most industries, not just retail. However, digital is still a largely amorphous concept, driven by the fact that much of the mainstream analyses of digital's impact only focus on the symptoms of digital. The underlying strategic dynamics of the digital economy are not widely understood or analyzed.

This chapter aims to address the inconsistent and limited understanding of digital's underlying dynamics. Elix-IRR believes that it is critical for all senior executives to understand, and then act upon, the digital forces that are shaping, and will continue to shape, their industries. Proficiency in the dynamics of digital is now a required corporate core competency.

1.3 DIGITAL PLATFORMS

Digital technology is disrupting established industries at an alarming rate, transforming the way consumers, suppliers and employees engage with brands and challenging the fundamental business models many businesses have historically relied upon. Organisations need to respond to this very real challenge by understanding the impact of changes in consumer behaviour, focusing on providing differentiating customer experiences and recognizing that IT is now a key strategic enabler for both realizing profitable growth and generating efficiencies for the organisation.

A critical component of the response and delivery of technology-driven business change is the digital platform. Standardizing processes, technologies and the collection, distribution and use of data in and around the organisation is central to supporting the delivery of greater value to customers. In this chapter, we summarize what a digital platform is, what is driving the need to develop them, and how to start planning to build one, using examples from a variety of industries.

1.4 THE RISE OF DIGITAL MONEY

The payments world is constantly evolving. So, which of the many nascent solutions are likely to disrupt the way in which payments are conducted in the future? And which global companies will lead the way? In this chapter, we examine how the payment industry has embraced digital payment methods and what enterprises should do to succeed in this new world.

1.1 CUSTOMERS ARE TRANSFORMING RETAIL

CUSTOMER-ORIENTATED INDUSTRIES ARE currently being transformed by digital trends, where the traditional business-customer relationship is disrupted by new technology and business model innovations.

Retail is at the heart of a digital revolution. However, this revolution is being led by consumers rather than directly by retailers as a result of retail-specific innovation.

Multichannel retailers today are operating in an industry where there are significant stakes to play for – survival – and the competitive landscape is in the middle of a seismic shift away from tradition.

CUSTOMERS ARE EMPOWERED BY INFORMATION AND TECHNOLOGY AT THEIR FINGERTIPS

Technology today allows the majority of us to access the internet through several connected devices in our homes, offices and on the move via our smartphones.

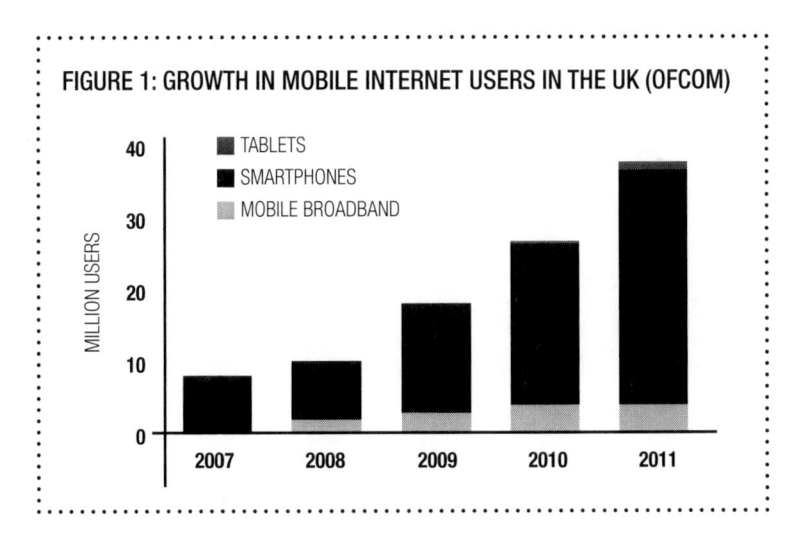

FIGURE 1: GROWTH IN MOBILE INTERNET USERS IN THE UK (OFCOM)

Among the technology hype, it can be hard to distinguish exactly how today's consumer prefers to engage with retailers. There are an ever-growing number of options as the purchase journey becomes more complex and the number of channels increases. Among the many options, there may be no strong preferences – customers simply seek choice, price and convenience.

CUSTOMERS ARE SHOPPING ON THEIR TERMS

Consumers are developing an expectation that they can shop and interact with retailers on demand, whatever the time of day or night.

In some general merchandise categories, nearly 90% (Econsultancy, 2013) of shoppers now claim to use more than one channel during a typical purchase. This behaviour varies dramatically for different categories, customer segments and for specific shopping "missions". The net result of this behaviour is a complex set of cross-channel customer journeys that retailers must understand, forecast and deliver 24 hours a day, every day.

TOMORROW'S RETAIL INDUSTRY WILL BE DRAMATICALLY DIFFERENT FROM TODAY'S:

- Today's pure plays will be truly multichannel with a physical presence based around convenience;
- Competition will escalate around innovations in service and customer experience;
- High streets will have a clear purpose as a showcase for fashion and innovation; and
- Supermarkets will have to offer a compelling service alternative to pure plays or they may lose out in general merchandise altogether.

DIGITAL RETAIL REVOLUTION

Figure 2 below describes a number of key drivers of change in retail, and discusses what the implications are for retailers.

FIGURE 2: DRIVERS OF RETAIL CHANGE

DRIVER OF CHANGE	WHY NOW?	IMPLICATIONS FOR RETAILERS
Accelerating Technology Customers have superfast internet technology in their pocket and expect to use it in all aspects of their lives	• Customers are immersed in a culture of constant connectivity • Function of mobile technology has evolved from a practical communications tool to a portal for sharing media, playing games, finding information and shopping	**Respond to a new pace of change** • Retailers are used to long technology cycles of 5–10 years but will now need to innovate in real time as consumers develop • The requirement now is to be close to the leading edge of technology and digital trends that do not originate in retail

Networked Consumers Customer loyalty is more easily swayed as switching is common to save money and follow latest trends	▪ Experiences are shared through social networking ▪ Trends arrive and disappear at high speed ▪ A vast amount of information is available to inform purchases ▪ Comparison sites make price highly transparent for branded goods	**Behave like consumers** ▪ Retailers and suppliers are no longer in control of fashion cycles – consumers create and communicate trends ▪ Retailers should pay attention to social networks and engage appropriately
New Business Models Customers have a digital mind-set and are open to new business models	▪ Businesses and consumers are becoming aware of the value of consumption data and are willing to trade ▪ A new generation of tech-savvy shoppers adapt more readily to change ▪ Automating routine activities such as the weekly shop is a more palatable concept	**Exploit data and new ways to pay** ▪ Retailers have a huge opportunity to gather valuable customer data through online relationships ▪ Retailers can establish effective cross-selling through product linking based on customer insight ▪ Opportunity to extract non-monetary value, i.e. information exchange via social media promotions
Trends Outside Retail Customers do not observe traditional industry boundaries	▪ Customers are "channel blind" and expect functionality, integration and consistency in all interactions with a brand ▪ Customer experience / service models developed by other industries (e.g., banking) now apply in retail ▪ Increasing diversification of product ranges is taking place, meaning that retailers are competing in new industries	**Don't get "tunnel vision"** ▪ Retailers should look beyond their industry to understand and adopt latest practices ▪ Opportunity to consider the wider customer experience across all channels, e.g., investing in online technology but not at the expense of stores

MOBILE IS AT THE CORE: SMARTPHONES ARE THE CATALYST FOR THE DIGITAL RETAIL REVOLUTION

Mobile technologies will be at the centre of the next stage of the digital retail revolution.

ACCELERATING INNOVATION CYCLES

Digital technology is evolving at pace and the general public have demonstrated a willingness to adopt and pay for cutting-edge technology. Mobile phone companies are releasing flagship devices on an annual basis and the propagation of computing power into tablets and other connected devices accelerates the innovation cycle.

Crucially, technology innovation is not limited to new hardware as creativity in developing new software and associated business models becomes one of the main drivers of change for digital retailers.

COMPUTING POWER IN YOUR POCKET

The computing power of the average smartphone now far outweighs the performance of a retail point-of-sale (POS) system and offers a live link to the internet. Mobile performance now allows for ever-more sophisticated applications that deliver a customer experience which retailers could not have provided with conventional infrastructure.

Forward-looking traditional retailers are ensuring that they are at the forefront of developing mobile retail applications. Otherwise, they run the risk of third-party solutions being brought into the digital retail ecosystem via mobiles, which would disrupt the current balance of power.

SEAMLESS CROSS-CHANNEL IDENTITY

Use of mobile devices in store offers a new opportunity for retailers to blur the line between online and offline sales. The mobile device can be used as an identifier to flag an online customer who is present in a physical store and target them with highly relevant and personalized promotions.

MARKETING AT THE RIGHT TIME

The capability to target customers in a highly localized and real-time way offers major benefits to both retailers and customers. Retailers can expect an increased marketing return on investment (ROI); spend can be more targeted and staff are able to identify their most valued customers as they enter the store environment, and provide an enhanced service. Customers can receive only the most relevant offers and personalized promotions, which reduces marketing noise and allows customers to modify their behaviour if it can bring them benefit.

For example, knowing that your favourite retailer has a branch nearby and has extended you a special offer would enable you to trade off the convenience of a closer rival retailer against the benefits offered by loyalty to your favourite retailer.

MOBILE WALLETS

Gartner expects the number of mobile transactions to increase to $600bn by 2016, up from $172bn in 2012 (Palmer, 2012).

The mobile phone payment market is slowly becoming saturated as banks, retailers and technology companies collaborate with mobile operators to give customers a truly digital experience in the store environment. Starbucks teamed up with Square and made its mark as the first coffee shop to give its customers a unique service. In August 2012, the largest US retailers, including Walmart, Target and Best Buy, announced plans to create a joint mobile wallet service (Palmer, 2012).

THE EVOLUTION OF ONLINE: THE JOURNEY FROM ONLINE ORDERS TO CUSTOMER EXPERIENCE

The digital retail experience has developed over time, and will continue to evolve at speed.

BUILDING AN ONLINE PRESENCE

The first phase of internet retailing saw most high-street names build an online presence very quickly and add simple ordering capabilities soon afterwards.

Retailers who failed to recognize the importance of new channels underinvested in technology platforms and digital marketing and were left standing still as competitors captured market share and gained an innovation advantage.

Many retailers today still bear the scars of the pioneering years of e-commerce when Amazon and other pure plays wrote the rulebook and set customer expectations to their advantage.

THE WEBSITE IS THE BIGGEST STORE

The second phase of e-commerce evolution saw revenues steadily rise as internet connectivity and confidence in security increased.

Developments in e-commerce saw an increasing number of retailers go online and extend their ranges, underpinned by improvements in stability and basic functionality of web platforms.

E-commerce steadily became more important to most retailers, and despite store sales still accounting for 90% of revenue on average, the website was seen as a large flagship store. Many retailers today are still trading websites where web platform and operations are based around these first-generation architectures.

GROWTH AND LINKING CHANNELS

Customers now expect seamless cross-channel experiences as standard (e.g., click and collect), which is forcing retailers to rebuild infrastructure to integrate web and store systems.

COMPLETE DIGITAL CUSTOMER EXPERIENCE

Customers today are digital and tend to cross channels without regard for the impact this has on how retailers choose to operate in these different channels.

Customer expectations are heavily influenced by other industries (banking, travel, insurance) and successful retailers need to be aware of any developments that may influence online or offline behaviours.

Social media has opened up a new dimension of interaction opportunities that allow the consumer a significant voice for feedback and give retailers insight into purchase decisions.

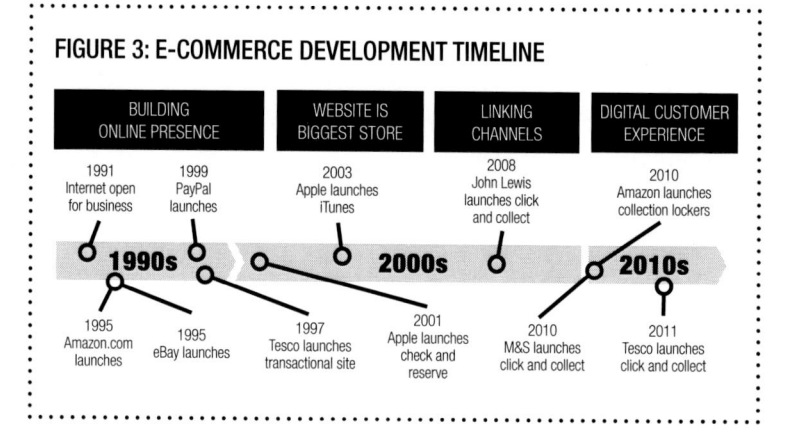

FIGURE 3: E-COMMERCE DEVELOPMENT TIMELINE

BUILDING ONLINE PRESENCE (1990s)	1991 Internet open for business; 1995 Amazon.com launches; 1995 eBay launches; 1999 PayPal launches
WEBSITE IS BIGGEST STORE (2000s)	1997 Tesco launches transactional site; 2001 Apple launches check and reserve; 2003 Apple launches iTunes
LINKING CHANNELS	2008 John Lewis launches click and collect; 2010 M&S launches click and collect
DIGITAL CUSTOMER EXPERIENCE (2010s)	2010 Amazon launches collection lockers; 2011 Tesco launches click and collect

THE ROLE OF THE STORE

Physical shops will remain but the economics are new. Despite the growth in online and mobile channels, the desire to see, touch and experience products before committing to purchase means that the store remains an important part of the customer journey. However, the traditional shop front has also changed through new technologies and consumer behaviours.

THE SHOWROOM STORE

The role of the store is shifting to become a showroom where consumers come to examine products and experience brand values without necessarily making a purchase. In fact, a Retail Week survey in late 2012 found that a quarter of UK consumers visited stores to see the products before comparing prices online (Goldfingle, 2013). The greatest challenge for retailers is to ensure that the consumer buys from them rather than a competitor, which means more than just focusing on price consistency across different channels. It requires value-enhancing convenience, innovation and service.

DIFFERENTIATION

Creative use of store space also brings an opportunity for the retailer to differentiate by enhancing the shopping experience (see Figure 4 for a selection of examples). Personalizing the store experience may be a good way to achieve this, for example by offering free Wi-Fi in store to

FIGURE 4: EXAMPLES OF DIGITAL RETAILING IN ACTION

EXAMPLE	DESCRIPTION
Burberry's flagship store blends the digital and physical retail environment in an immersive brand experience	Fitting the store with sofas and iPads offers comfort in a stylish setting. The store **brings alive the online environment**, appealing to the customer's senses while providing **continuity with the web format** and meeting the online shopper's **expectations on immediacy**. Educating customers about buying online may also **encourage them to purchase more often from the website** when they are away from a store (Batten, 2012)
The John Lewis app allows the customer to access enhanced product information on their phone	Allows customers to scan products on their mobile phones to access enhanced product information. The service offers a new dimension for interacting with products through online content such as **videos and reviews** (John Lewis, 2013)
Tesco's mobile app helps customers locate in-store products	Brings the **habit of online navigation into the store context** – offers **cross-selling opportunities** through effective product linking (Williams, 2011)
Virgin Media has opened a new store with an interactive video wall	Makes **entertainment retail stimulating at the point of purchase** – allowing customers to play, browse, watch and interact with products and services, fits the brand and attracts new customers (Withers, 2013)

identify returning consumers and offer them relevant promotions or an enhanced service.

HOW CAN RETAILERS STAY AHEAD?

The pace of change in the digital world means that the retail industry will not always be the leader of customer experience innovation across all industries. However, retailers will need to remain at the forefront of change since customer expectations are driven by digital brands outside of retail, and innovations are likely to be quickly adopted by their competitors.

FIGURE 5: HOW RETAILERS CAN STAY AHEAD

Take a customer rather than a channel view on the operating model	▪ Keep the customer experience as the foundation of the operating model – customers do not see channels, they see a brand ▪ Understand expectations and measure behaviours ▪ Gather customer data to drive cross-channel analytics
Define the company's brand proposition clearly and communicate to the customer	▪ Keep sight of basic retail fundamentals and put customer needs at the core of the brand proposition ▪ Ensure that brand values are clearly communicated consistently across all channels
Capitalize on multichannel capabilities while there is still an advantage	▪ Use location and proximity to customers as an advantage over online-only retailers for a quality personal interaction ▪ Focus on physical retail fundamentals – online-only retailers are inexperienced at managing physical stores
Stay close to the technology edge, but stay focused on the customer, not the technology	▪ Customers adopt new technologies faster than retailers ▪ Respond quickly to trends rather than running at the "bleeding edge"

KEY TAKEAWAYS:

1. Customer expectations have shifted dramatically as a result of technology change
2. Building a seamless experience across channels is increasingly important
3. Mobile computing will be at the heart of future retail developments

1.2 DIGITAL'S UNDERLYING DYNAMICS

THE TERM "DIGITAL" and its related trends are often reported upon and discussed in today's media; the explosion of social media, the rise of the smartphone, the promise of big data (and little data), the flexibility of the Cloud, the imperative of multichannel, the need for customer-centricity and the demise of high-street retailers such as HMV, Jessops and Blockbuster are very well publicized.

Digital technology, and innovative business models built around such technology, are topical and are significantly impacting most industries, not just retail.

However, digital is still a largely amorphous concept, driven by the fact that much of the mainstream analyses of digital's impact only focus on the symptoms of digital. The underlying strategic dynamics of the digital economy are not widely understood or analyzed.

THE GROWTH OF THE DIGITAL ECONOMY

By 2016, the digital economy of the G20 is predicted to be valued at $4.2 trillion; making it larger than the German economy (The Boston Consulting Group, 2012). Analysts collectively expect this growth to continue into the future. While the internet itself dates back to the 1960s, the World Wide Web, which effectively made the internet accessible to organisations and individuals, is only just over 20 years old. Over those 20 years, we have witnessed the set of business applications of the "web" evolve as companies experimented with how to monetize the innovative communication technology.

Early use of the web was typified by brochureware websites, whereby companies adopted the same marketing mentality as was relevant to broadcast technology such as radio and television. In the mid-to-late 1990s digital products began to emerge, such as MP3 music files. Next came e-commerce, whereby the profound commercial applicability of the web was experienced, primarily by retailers, in the early 2000s. In 2007, Apple's iPhone was released. This category-defining smartphone heralded a new wave of technology-driven business innovation. Companies could now have meaningful interactions with their customers regardless of time or place. Terms such as "digital", "digital natives", "digital business models", "digital strategy" and "digital transformation" became commonplace in industries.

This 20-year evolution of business use of the web will not end here. Over the next 20 years and beyond, we shall witness further innovative applications of web technology. Industry structures shall change.

WHAT IS "DIGITAL"?

- "Digital", in the contemporary sense, lacks a specific, agreed-upon definition.
- Originally "digital" referred to data represented in a series of discrete values – specifically 1s and 0s. The primary benefit of this form of data representation is that data can be stored and transmitted easily using wired and wireless technology. This observation is the technical basis of the digital economy. Products and services are moving from physical entities to digital entities (e.g., books, music, insurance cover) that can be produced, stored and distributed at low cost.
- Today "digital" is largely used as a catch all phrase to encompass many aspects of the digital economy; for example, mobile, social, data, customer behaviour and business models.
- Elix-IRR believes that "digital", as a term, will be less frequently used over the coming years. "Digital" will simply be a fundamental element of good business practice. Every company will become a digital company.

Companies shall rise and fall as the nature of industry competition changes. From payments to manufacturing, from government to retail, all industries need to come to terms with the digital economy, and the new forms of opportunity and competition that this economy brings. Progressive digital businesses, built on web technologies and new approaches to delivering customer value, will entirely change competitive landscapes.

FOUR OBSERVATIONS ON DIGITAL'S STRATEGIC DYNAMICS:

To truly understand digital's impact on industries, the following observations are critical:

1. **THE RISE OF A NEW VALUE EXCHANGE:** Digital enables a new value exchange between a customer and a company; personal information is a new form of currency (and a new source of business innovation);
2. **THE EROSION OF BARRIERS TO ENTRY:** Traditional industry barriers to entry are being eroded by technology-based business models resulting in historically dominant organisations having to reconsider how they deliver value;
3. **THE EMERGENCE OF TRANSIENT STRATEGY:** With protective industry barriers to entry eroding, and incumbents facing significant structural change, transient, exploratory business strategies will become ever more crucial; and
4. **THE NEED FOR ADAPTABLE OPERATIONS:** With business strategies

becoming transient, business model innovation and an adaptable operating model are critical to support dynamic competition in the digital economy.

These four observations, which are elaborated upon throughout this chapter, begin to explain why business executives are compelled to look beyond traditional management methods and concepts and reconsider how best to compete in the digital economy.

THE RISE OF A NEW VALUE EXCHANGE

The digital economy produces vast swathes of data. So much so that IBM estimates that 90% of all data that exists globally was created in the last 2 years (IBM, 2012). Of this big data, personal information has undeniably emerged as the data type with the most latent value. In fact, personal information has become a new form of currency in the digital economy. Digital giants, such as Facebook and Google, are prime examples of organisations who inherently understand this; they have both built global businesses by monetizing access to vast amounts of personal information (via the provision of targeted advertising services). However, such success hinges on understanding the new value exchange. Traditional companies, with aspirations of growth in the digital economy, are beginning to appreciate the value of personal information and master the new value exchange.

PERSONAL INFORMATION IN ADDITION TO MONEY

The traditional value exchange between a customer and a company – money in exchange for a product or service – is evolving. In the digital economy, personal information is now embedded at the core of the exchange. In addition to money, a typical customer shares their personal information as a critical part of the value exchange. In turn, the company is compelled to use that personal information to provide an enhanced, personalized product or service that helps the customer achieve their overarching desire. This is a simple observation, but the business implications are immense.

A NEW FOCUS FOR INNOVATION

With access to personal information, and a mandate to use that information in the interest of the customer, digital companies are empowered to innovate around the customer's "jobs to be done". With some exceptions, most customers do not really desire a generic product or service; instead, they require the product or service to achieve something more substantial yet elusive. For example, customers may want "to stay healthy", "to find love", "to learn", "to look fashionable", "to retire early" or simply "to relax and be entertained". With ready access to a flow of personal information and with a better understanding of what customers truly desire, digital companies align their value propositions with their customers' true desires. This is the essence of the digital value exchange, the digital economy and the reason why digital poses an existential threat to the old paradigm of companies simply providing products and services to their customers.

FROM "CONSUMER" TO "INDIVIDUAL"

With personal information, the value exchange has the potential to become more emotional, more intimate. An opportunity is presented to companies to refocus their value propositions on customers' true desires. Supported by technology, "consumers" can be treated as "individuals" once again. The opportunity for the company to re-establish a more intimate customer relationship, differentiate and achieve a superior level of loyalty is compelling. Somewhat ironically, the superior use of technology can help companies return to their roots and engage with customers in a more personal, meaningful manner.

Next, this chapter showcases examples of how technology-native firms and more traditional firms have innovated with the new value exchange by aligning their value propositions with customers' true objectives.

> ### WARNING: THE ABUSE OF PERSONAL INFORMATION
>
> There is a growing unease with online firms' use of personal information. Many internet revenue models are based on personal information-fuelled advertising, resulting in near-ubiquitous, intrusive online advertising. Privacy incidents (e.g., the US PRISM programme) draw attention to the risk of personal information leaks. This highlights the importance to firms of ensuring that the new digital value exchange is used in the interest of the customer, supporting their desired jobs to be done and growing loyalty.

EXAMPLE APPLICATIONS OF DIGITAL'S NEW VALUE EXCHANGE

A primary consideration of the traditional concept of strategy is the erection of defensible barriers to entry. Companies erect and manage barriers to deter competition and to protect their industries' profitability. These barriers served industry profitability well for decades. However, digital technologies, wrapped in innovative business models, are attacking

FIGURE 6: EXAMPLE APPLICATIONS OF DIGITAL'S NEW VALUE EXCHANGE

NIKE+
The Nike+ concept was designed to help Nike's customers "get fit" through the innovative combination of sportswear, device technology, social technology, data algorithms and personal information. While exercising, various sensors capture the athlete's movement and personal performance information. This information, coupled with other athlete information including weight, age and resting heart rate, is used to calculate performance statistics using proprietary Nike algorithms. Nike provide a social platform for athletes to analyze their performance and to instil a sense of community competition and collaboration.

This tech-driven innovation has enabled Nike to reduce its reliance on marketing to retain a connection with its customers. Nike+, and a flow of personal information, enables Nike to grow customer loyalty, not around marketing messages, but around helping customers achieve their athletic goals. Nike's inherent understanding of the digital value exchange enabled the company to move from a product focus to an experience focus.

JOHN DEERE FARMSIGHT
"Personal information" need not necessarily be limited to an actual person. For example, John Deere Farmsight is a suite of technology-based products and services that collectively help farmers "increase farming output". Farming machinery, equipped with John Deere's JDLink wireless technology, are permanently connected to the internet and can be monitored remotely via computers, tablets and smartphones. Various sensors provide machine data on the machine's location, instrumentation and control systems. John Deere dealers, who are granted access to this machine data as part of the "value exchange", can proactively diagnose and optimize farm machinery, assist farmers, coordinate fleets and use field data for better analysis.

John Deere has moved beyond the provision of farming basic products and services. They have innovated with the digital value exchange using data and technology to help farmers optimize the use of their machinery and their farming output.

these barriers to entry and reducing industry profitability. Industries are increasingly exposed to new forms of technology-enabled competition, leading to structural industry changes. This is commonly referred to as "digital disruption".

THE EXPANSION OF COMPETITOR SETS
Industry incumbents face new forms of technology-based competition

MIDATA

Acknowledging the emergence of digital's new value exchange, and the latent value in personal data, the UK Government established the "midata" initiative to "give the power of consumer data back to consumers themselves". Initially, the initiative focused on giving individuals better access, and control over, the electronic personal data that companies hold about them.

However, in 2013, the Government established a related initiative to nurture business innovation with personal data, while providing oversight and assurance that this initiative was respectful of personal privacy and confidentiality concerns. In conjunction with cross-industry organisations such as BBC, npower and Telefonica, the "midata Innovation Lab" was established. This lab built a rich personal dataset (using private sector, public sector and personal information from 1,000 individuals) and invited businesses to innovate with this data set and provide new, innovative services that support the customers' objectives. The initial phase of the midata Innovation Lab initiative was completed in late 2013.

GOOGLE NOW

Google Now is an "intelligent personal assistant" with a significant disruptive potential. Google has access to a veritable treasure trove of user information. Google Now uses that information and recognizes repeated actions and information trends (common locations, repeated calendar appointments, search queries, etc.) to display very relevant information to the user. As would be expected of a personal assistant, the Google Now application supports users across many facets of their lives – including notifying them of upcoming meetings, informing them of birthdays, calculating the fastest commuting routes, informing them of new potentially interesting movies, suggesting local events, providing scores from sporting events and forecasting the weather.

What makes Google Now so impressive is that much of these information updates can be provided proactively by the application. Google's historical search capabilities are reactive, but Google Now represents a move to the provision of proactive services using the new value exchange.

from traditional competitors, adjacent industries and start-ups. For most industries, this is not just a threat, it is happening right now; retail, telecoms, media, financial services, travel, recruitment, education and even manufacturing, amongst many other industry sectors, are currently experiencing varying degrees of disruption.

A new generation of disruption-minded individuals has emerged who are armed with a superior understanding of internet technologies, and how personal information is at the core of digital's value exchange. Undeterred by barriers to entry, these individuals, in both traditional and digital firms, are re-writing how value is created and how business models are structured.

THE RISK OF INACTION

The implications of this disruption are stark. Companies are compelled to use technology to innovate with their business models. Customers expect companies to "go digital", while shareholders expect companies to stay relevant and grow. Those companies who fail to act, and who rely on an assumption that barriers to entry will protect their profitability, face a future of market irrelevance and financial decline.

PLATFORMS: A NEW BARRIER TO ENTRY

While technology and innovative business models do contribute to the erosion of traditional barriers to entry, the concept of these barriers is still very applicable to business strategy. In fact, Elix-IRR suggests that a new type of barrier to entry has been introduced – the platform. The four iconic digital companies – Google, Facebook, Amazon and Apple – all protect their dominant industry positions through the establishment of multi-sided platforms. Google provides a multi-sided platform for individuals to find information, and for advertisers to find those individuals. Facebook provides a platform for individuals to interact with each other, and for advertisers to join in that interaction. Amazon provides a platform to connect buyers and sellers. Apple provides a platform, built around iTunes, to provide customers with access to media (such as apps, videos and music), and to provide media producers with access to those customers. The scale of each of these platforms inhibits competition. Elix-IRR also believes that other industries will progress towards platform competition in the future. For example, the dominant retail bank of the future may achieve, and sustain, its success through the provision of a banking platform that connects the bank, its customers, 3rd-party companies and 4th-party companies that represent customers.

FIGURE 7: HOW DIGITAL IS ERODING BARRIERS TO ENTRY

BARRIER TO ENTRY	HOW DIGITAL IS ERODING THE BARRIER TO ENTRY	INDUSTRY EXAMPLE
Supply-side economies of scale	In part driven by Cloud technology and concepts such as Moore's Law*, technology costs are falling rapidly. Firms who can build business models around cost-effective internet technology can undermine the supply-side cost advantages of traditional competitors. * Moore's Law predicts that the number of transistors per square inch on integrated circuits will double for the foreseeable year. This prediction is the basis of technology's continuing performance improvement and relative cost decrease	**Music Distribution** Apple iTunes, the music distribution platform, has demonstrated how technology can undercut many of the supply-side cost advantages enjoyed by traditional music retailers. Apple envisaged, and built, a new approach to music distribution, thereby avoiding like-for-like competition with incumbent physical retailers who incorrectly assumed their scale afforded them a supply-side cost advantage.
Demand-side benefits of scale	In the digital economy, positive network effects are amplified by the ability of companies to rapidly acquire customers via technology channels. The rate of acquisition, and the global reach of digital companies, has the potential to eclipse the networks established by traditional firms. Incumbents who are dependent on network effects can see their advantage rapidly eroded.	**Telecommunications** Whatsapp, the Over the Top (OTT) telecommunications messaging service, has grown to service over 250 million monthly active users within 4 years of inception, with the attractiveness of the Whatsapp service increasing with every new user. Remarkably, Whatsapp achieved this user growth with no marketing budget. Whatsapp also undermines telecommunications' supply-side cost advantage through an asymmetric business model (relative to incumbent infrastructure-owning telecoms companies), and using technology to reduce Whatsapp's marginal cost of customer service to near-zero.
Customer switching costs	As products and services are digitized, switching costs are reduced. In the digital economy switching can be as easy as downloading a different app or visiting a different website. Price comparison and customer review websites, such as Gocompare.com and TripAdvisor, aid user discovery and catalyze switching.	**Car Insurance** The initial digitization of the car insurance sector took the form of online distribution. Consumers could purchase insurance products via new channels. This allowed aggregator websites, such as Gocompare.com and comparethemarket.com, to offer consumers comparison services across insurance providers. In turn, the increase in industry price transparency has led to an increase in customer switching and price-based competition.

Capital intensity	With technology costs reducing, the investment required to enter an industry, or grow within an industry, with a technology-based business model is significantly reduced. In some circumstances, capital investments can be largely avoided.	**News Publishing** Traditional news publishing is a very capital-intensive business, largely driven by the need to produce and distribute paper-based news. These capital needs placed a heavy reliance on newspaper advertising. In contrast, online-only "news organisations", ranging from Twitter to the MailOnline, have more favourable capital intensity ratios and can potentially scale operations disproportionately to their capital costs.
Distributor agreements	The internet, and resulting internet-enabled devices such as smartphones, has offered firms a platform to "go direct" to customers; thereby bypassing entrenched distribution agreements. In many industries, where technology innovation is primarily limited to using digital as a channel, distribution is a fiercely competed area. Aggregator websites and online market places have also arisen to intensify distribution-based competition.	**Leisure Travel** The travel industry has historically relied on high-street travel agents and call centres to sell travel products. While the supply chain had been digitized by CRS (Central Reservation System) and GDS (Global Distribution System) technology, the demand side of the distribution chain was largely physical. The emergence of the internet has changed that. Distribution barriers to entry dropped and online travel agents (OTAs), such as Expedia, Booking.com and Orbitz, have led to travel agents being disintermediated for many types of travel products. Travel suppliers, such as airlines and hoteliers, have also used the internet to distribute directly to customers and avoid margin erosion.
Predatory pricing	Technology-enabled companies can typically reduce their marginal costs below those of their more traditional competitors. Technology can provide a firm with an ability to scale revenues disproportionately to costs. This gives them the ability to explore innovative revenue models and offer free, or nearly free, products and services. Competitors with primarily physical assets struggle to compete.	**Private Banking** Wealthfront, a disruptive, software-based wealth management company, uses technology and algorithms to reduce their customer servicing costs significantly – relative to traditional private banks and wealth management companies. Investor relationships are largely automated, yet customized, using technology and algorithms to help scale investment advice. As a result of this low marginal cost, Wealthfront can offer their customers very low investment fees that undercut competitors.

THE EMERGENCE OF TRANSIENT STRATEGY

With barriers to entry eroding, digital-savvy firms look for opportunities to change the basis of competition in industries – in their own favour. Initially, incumbent firms disregard the disruptive threat – as HMV initially disregarded the disruptive threat of Apple's iTunes. However, as disruptive technologies improve and gain market traction, incumbent firms slowly come to the realization that their previously relied upon strategies and competitive advantages are, in fact, not sustainable. As a result of having previously underestimated disruptive business models, incumbents often lack the time or financial resources to transform, and fail to adapt to the new basis of industry competition. The very real consequences of disruption are evident – in addition to HMV, other retailers such as Jessops, Dixons and Blockbuster are no longer going concerns.

CORPORATE RIGIDITY

In each of the above examples, the failed organisations effectively hardwired many aspects of their business model in the belief that they could rely on a set of barriers to entry built to protect a narrow view of the basis of industry competition. Often, as management becomes complacent to new opportunities for value creation and business model innovation, firms focus their resources on operational improvements and incremental innovations. Historically, such resource focuses served firms moderately well. However, in the digital economy these narrow focuses represent a failure to invest in the new bases of industry competition and expose the firm to the threat of disruption.

For example, at the height of HMV's success, the company had over 300 stores throughout the UK and Ireland. This distribution network, one of HMV's primary barriers to entry, was erected, and continuously invested in, under an assumption that the basis of competition in media distribution was access to physical retail outlets. Apple assumed otherwise.

DISRUPTION IS PROVING TO BE ITERATIVE

One-off business model innovation might have saved certain disrupted firms; however, industry disruption is proving to be iterative. Just as Apple helped disrupt HMV and the old physical approach to music distribution, Apple are now being disrupted by a subscription-based economic model to charge for music (as practised by Spotify). Just as high-street travel agents were disrupted by online travel agents, a new breed of peer-to-peer travel accommodation providers, such as AirBnB, are now "re-disrupting" the travel distribution sector. The very same eroded barriers to entry, which allowed disruptive companies to transform an industry, also expose those disruptive companies to further disruption. Digital is catalyzing not just disruption, but multiple waves of disruption.

THE NEED FOR TRANSIENT STRATEGIES

The strategic implications of iterative disruption are profound; strategy definition is becoming a transient initiative. In the face of iterative disruption, transient business strategies, supported by adaptable operating models, are the key to remaining relevant in an industry. Firms' competitive landscapes are becoming very diverse – with threats stemming from previously unconsidered sources. The boundaries between industries are becoming blurred – as evidenced by telecom operators' attempts to control the emerging mobile payments industry. To forward-thinking firms, opportunities, and not just threats, will also be diverse. To benefit from these opportunities, firms need to be able to identify, enter, exploit and leave markets in an agile manner. The ability for firms to follow transient strategies, supported by adaptable operating models, is crucial in the digital economy.

THE NEED FOR ADAPTABLE OPERATIONS

Corporate survival and profitable growth in the digital economy is increasingly dependent on a firm's ability to develop transient strategies. Naturally, those transient strategies must be underpinned by the firm's operating model. Effectively, the operating model must be able to adapt to support an evolving portfolio of business objectives and opportunities, with those opportunities guided by the evolving bases of industry competition.

For example, HBO, the premium American broadcaster, is following a transient strategy in OTT-based broadcasting. It is evolving its operating model to support its new HBO Go service. The HBO operating model now supports both traditional cable/satellite-based broadcasting along with OTT broadcasting. Similarly, mobile telecommunications provider O2, facing ongoing commoditization of its core voice, SMS and data services, is pursuing a portfolio of "digital services" strategies. These services, including the O2 wallet, TU Go VOIP services, O2 Tracks, and Priority Moments, are arguably the strategic equivalent of investment portfolio management, whereby certain initiatives will prove successful and others will prove not to be so.

Elix-IRR believes that operating model adaptability is crucial to underpin the success of such transient strategies. In contrast, as proven by HMV, operating model rigidity hinders the required evolution of a company and jeopardizes its market position.

ADAPTABLE OPERATING MODEL CHARACTERISTICS

An adaptable operating model has different characteristics depending on the firm and industry in question. However, there are definite themes across firms, some of which are detailed below:

- **LEADERSHIP:** Strong leadership is critical to move from a rigid operating model to an adaptive operating model. Leaders must not only articulate a vision, but be clear and adamant in defining what the operating model should, and should not, support.
- **BUSINESS CAPABILITIES:** Core business capabilities should be modular, in support of transient strategies. Non-core business capabilities can be outsourced.
- **MULTIPLE OPERATING MODELS:** To simultaneously support multiple transient strategies, multiple operating models may be required. The balance between integrating and autonomously operating these models must be clear – to ensure the independent success of each model.
- **PEOPLE:** The employee base must be skilled not just in operating existing functions but in creating functions, shutting down functions and delivering change across functions.
- **GOVERNANCE:** Organisational resources must be allocated to promote agility and not solely to reinforce current advantages.
- **ORGANISATION:** The organisation must be structured to support the entire business unit lifecycle – launch, operation and shut-down. Product-oriented silos should be broken down in favour of customer-orientation.
- **INVESTMENT MANAGEMENT:** Investment decisions must not solely be based on traditional financial metrics, such as Net Present Value, which downplay the cost of not investing in innovation and new capabilities.
- **INNOVATION:** Processes must be in place to nurture both sustaining and disruptive innovation possibilities.
- **TECHNOLOGY:** The technology platform should be modular, extensible and reusable to support a portfolio of business opportunities.
- **DIGITAL:** And of course, innovation, analytics, partnership, collaboration and multichannel capabilities – via technology – should be core competencies.

Elix-IRR believe that these, and other adaptable operating model characteristics, are critical in enabling firms to flex their operating model to stay relevant in the face of uncertain competition and transient advantages.

FIGURE 8: CONCLUSIONS

Digital is often misunderstood	While very topical and often reported upon, digital lacks a clear definition and is largely misunderstood. Most business practitioners can speak to the symptoms of digital, but few can explain the underlying strategic dynamics.
Business innovation on internet technologies will continue	The World Wide Web enabled businesses to commercialize the internet. Since the 1990s we have seen that commercialization leads to the growth of the digital economy. This economy will continue to grow. Industries will change. Companies shall fall, while others shall rise.
The rise of a new value exchange	A new digital value exchange, based on personal information, has emerged. The value exchange promotes a more emotional connection between a customer and a firm; if the firm uses personal information to help customers achieve something they truly care about.
The erosion of barriers to entry	Traditional barriers to entry are under attack from technology-based business models. Historical industry protective mechanisms are falling, leaving industries open to iterative disruption – a shift in the basis of competition and the structure of industries.
The emergence of transient strategy	As barriers to entry are eroded, competitive advantages and strategies are no longer sustainable. To stay relevant in their increasingly digitized markets, incumbent companies are exploring transient strategic initiatives.
The need for adaptable operations	As transient business strategies become the norm, the expectation is that adaptable operating models support business growth. Adaptable operating models are increasingly required for success in the digital economy.

CONCLUSIONS

The digital economy offers profound opportunities for growth. However, availing of such opportunities, and avoiding the disruptive impact of the digital economy, requires that your organisation has a clear vision that guides coordinated change across both your revenue and operating model. Elix-IRR can help articulate a pragmatic vision for your organisation, deliver appropriate changes to your operating model to increase your adaptability, and guide and coordinate change. Our consultants have deep experience in the digital economy from digital strategy to the creation of innovation capabilities, from programme design to organisation model restructuring.

KEY TAKEAWAYS:

1. Personal information is a new form of currency and source of business innovation
2. Industries' historical protection mechanisms are under attack
3. Facing increasing and repeated industry disruption, business model innovation in support of transient strategies is crucial
4. As strategies and opportunities become more and more transient, business' underlying operating models must be highly adaptable

1.3 DIGITAL PLATFORMS

THIS CHAPTER DISCUSSES a critical component of technology-driven business change – the digital platform.

We summarize what a digital platform is, what is driving the need to develop one, and how to start planning to build one, using examples from a variety of industries.

INTRODUCING DIGITAL DISRUPTION

Emerging technologies are continuing to disrupt established markets and traditional business models:

- Barriers to entry in many industries have decreased as the tools and infrastructure to compete with established businesses have become freely available (for example, anyone can now set up a shop on eBay, raise funding for a film via Kickstarter or self-publish a book on Create Space for a fraction of the capital required two decades ago);
- Consumers are more connected than ever before, and this is creating explosive demand for digital products and services. It took 30 years to connect the first 2 billion people to the internet. It will take less than seven to connect the next 2 billion (Arthur, 2013);
- Digital products and services can be launched to market at increasing speed (at its launch in July 2008, there were 800 apps available to download from the iPhone App Store. In July 2013, there were over 900,000, with 375,000 of those native to iPad (Costello, 2013);
- Greater levels of automation are reducing the scale of human intervention required to perform complex tasks, whilst speeding up the product development process. For example, companies such as Nike and Adidas have embraced 3D printing to accelerate the shoemaking process. Adidas recently reported that it has reduced the time it takes to evaluate new prototypes from 4-6 weeks to 1-2 days (Jopson, 2013); and
- The processing power of computing has now reached a level where real-time capture and analysis of large and complex data sets is a reality, meaning the timeframe for making business critical decisions has reduced markedly. Companies such as GE are now able to monitor the performance of industrial equipment using sensors that transmit performance data in real time (Waters, 2013) (see the General Electric case study in Figure 8 for an example).

As a result of these and other developments, customers now expect better functionality from the products and services they buy and consume. In retail, for instance, more personalized service, greater choice and faster delivery times are all attributes consumers are demanding. This is changing the response required by modern retail businesses.

Consequently, IT divisions across all industries are being asked to develop and deliver more effective and efficient digital platforms to support rapidly evolving expectations. However, in order to do this, they need to redefine complex processes, shake up traditional organisational structures and replace the legacy "spaghetti" of poorly integrated systems.

For the purposes of this discussion, we use the term "digital platform" to refer to:

"The sum of the integrated processes and digital technologies that support and channel data around an organisation."

WHAT IS DRIVING THE NEED TO DEVELOP A DIGITAL PLATFORM?

There are a number of factors driving businesses to consider investing in the development of a digital platform.

THE NEED TO RESPOND TO SHIFTS IN CONSUMER BEHAVIOUR

As previously identified, the way in which we consume products and services has undergone a revolution. Consumers have become data hungry, demanding more information via digitally connected devices and mobile applications than ever before.

For instance, analysts have estimated that global mobile handset data traffic will rise by approximately 300% by 2017, from 5 exabytes (an exabyte is a billion gigabytes) in 2012 to 21 exabytes in 2017 (see Figure 9 overleaf). This will be driven primarily by video streaming and web browsing (Lunden, 2013).

Add into this equation the increasing thirst for consumer "self-quantification" in the form of technologies that monitor health, sports performance and all manner of other daily activities, and the result is that businesses need to develop new platforms and services to cope with exponential consumer demand for data.

Complementary to this shift in consumption patterns is a shift in how we engage with brands and businesses. Consumers have moved from expecting a transactional relationship to demanding a more engaging and interactive experience. As a consequence, the line between what is a product and what is a service has blurred. A classic example is Nike's + application, which has transformed the running shoe into an interactive experience by using a digital platform to manage users' performance data and to facilitate engagement with a wider community.

A disruptive side effect of this phenomenon is the blurring of traditional industry definitions. Telecoms businesses now provide banking services, retailers have become media businesses, and manufacturers are becoming data service providers. As a result, businesses are having to redefine the space in which they compete.

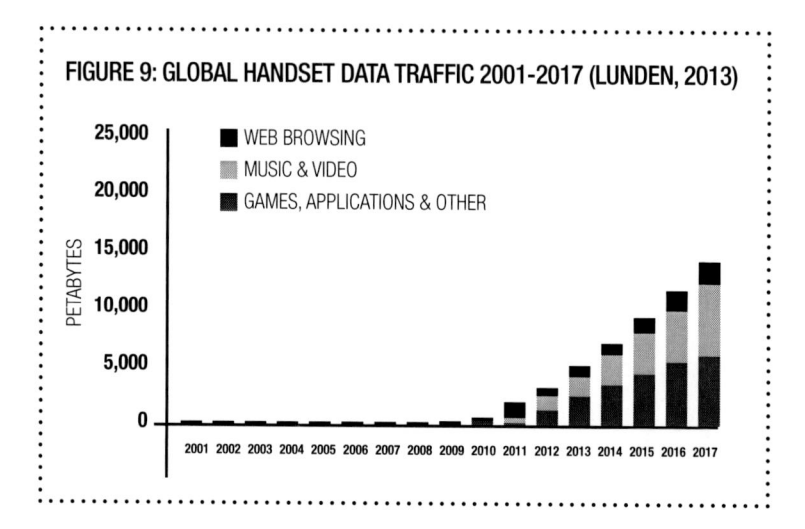

FIGURE 9: GLOBAL HANDSET DATA TRAFFIC 2001-2017 (LUNDEN, 2013)

THE NEED TO PROVIDE CUSTOMERS WITH A BETTER EXPERIENCE

Providing customers – whether business-to-consumer (B2C) or business-to-business (B2B) – with a smooth and integrated experience is increasingly seen as a "must-have". Customers now expect to be able to access digital content and services on demand, order products at any time of day and perform routine activities (such as banking or travel booking) from connected digital devices in any location around the world.

In order to deliver these experiences effectively, businesses need to be able to provide customers with a digital platform that incorporates services such as secure single sign-on, device-agnostic access to content, search tools, secure mobile payment gateways and a host of other building blocks associated with the delivery of an integrated customer experience. Without these, the experience is frustrating, clunky and inconsistent, and ultimately results in dissatisfaction, defection and lost revenue. Figure 10 overleaf presents the case study of the crowdfunding website Kickstarter, a good example of a digital platform that provides a slick and frictionless user experience.

FIGURE 10: KICKSTARTER DIGITAL PLATFORM CASE STUDY

CASE STUDY 1:

Kickstarter uses a digital platform to respond to the funding needs of the creative community

Background
- Kickstarter is a crowdfunding platform that provides funding access to the creative community.
- Since its launch in 2009, more than 4.5 million people have funded over 45,000 creative projects, pledging over $725 million in the process. (Kickstarter, Inc., 2013).

Challenge
- Creative projects are notoriously difficult to fund, often because of the difficulty associated with calculating their return on investment (ROI).
- Kickstarter and other reward-based crowdfunding specialists promise no ROI. Instead the "creators" offer specific rewards based on the sum committed from the "backer". The "creators" are then able to manage their campaigns for funding via the website and mobile applications.

Digital Response
- The Kickstarter digital platform provides its users with a virtually frictionless technology experience, enabling the delivery of an investment funding service to customers in both the US and UK, and is in the process of scaling to other countries.
- Central to the success of the platform is the ease with which creators and backers can create and track projects, and the key metrics relating to these.
- In 2012 Kickstarter further improved its digital platform when it launched a mobile application.

A SHIFT IN THE ROLE OF IT

As a result of these pressures, IT has continued to move from being viewed as a support function and cost centre, primarily responsible for "keeping the lights on", to a strategic asset at the forefront of enabling profitable growth through exploiting digital platforms.

Whilst the strategic importance of IT is generally not disputed, many IT organisations, and the systems and processes that support them, have suffered from a lack of clear strategic direction, and as a result, are often not in a position to support the wider digital ambitions of the business. In many cases organisations have reached a tipping point whereby there is now a chronic need to overhaul how IT operates in order to deliver their digital vision.

THE DRIVE FOR EFFICIENCY

Whilst digital platforms can create a host of new revenue-generating products and service opportunities, an equally important but sometimes overlooked benefit is the ability to deliver greater efficiencies for the organisation.

Legacy technology platforms frequently suffer from process bottlenecks caused by "manual" interventions or workarounds whereby certain activities can often only be executed at specific times or by certain individuals. Digital platforms can help to release these bottlenecks by introducing intelligent automation, speeding up the time it takes to perform tasks and driving down the cost of the production and the delivery of products and services.

A good example of how digital has enabled efficiencies in health services is the digitization of X-rays, using a picture archiving and communication (PACS) systems. Where previously a conventional radiological film required hard copy X-rays to be taken, processed, filed, stored and retrieved, modern PACS systems rely on the digital transmission of X-rays. This has resulted in large efficiencies from electronic, rather than manual, data handling. Images are available day or night anywhere within a hospital (or indeed outside if necessary), can be viewed in multiple locations at once, can be manipulated with computer-based tools and can be easily searched and retrieved from storage using the metadata associated with the images (for example, using patient details, dates or type of injury) (Strickland, 2000).

Another efficiency associated with digital platforms relates to the ability to do more with less. As an example, retailers once had to rely on a large network of stores and employees to reach their customer base, with the associated large fixed cost base. In a digital world, retailers can instead use websites and mobile applications that provide access to more customers, at any point in the day, with no restrictions on the amount of times a customer might visit, and without the need for thousands of employees or a network of branches.

The cost of one more customer visit is practically zero in a digital world. Therefore, the normal restrictions associated with the physical environment do not apply (for example, range restrictions, parking, queues at tills or for customer services).

In addition, the increased uptake of software-as-a-service (SaaS) licencing models, and the rapid growth of freeware and open-source software, has enabled businesses to overcome previous barriers associated with the high costs of software development and maintenance.

For example, in 3D printing digital designs for products can be stored on a server, and then printed off locally as required. Classic car restorers can now even reverse engineer in order to create parts for cars which would previously have had to be either tracked down or built by specialists (Economist, 2013).

As these examples illustrate, digital platforms can deliver efficiencies by reducing manual intervention, reducing fixed costs and accelerating the speed with which a business can perform various activities.

FIGURE 11: GENERAL ELECTRIC DIGITAL PLATFORM CASE STUDY

CASE STUDY 2:

General Electric uses a digital platform to deliver data services

Background
- General Electric (GE) is a global infrastructure, finance and media company which has been innovating for over 130 years (General Electric Company, 2013).
- GE works across industries as diverse as aviation, healthcare, oil and gas, rail and many others. GE has re-invented itself over the years by continually diversifying its business model, the solutions it provides and the industries it operates in.

Challenge
- Complex industrial equipment requires careful monitoring in order to ensure operation within predefined safety parameters.
- In addition, understanding how equipment performs in different environments and under different stresses helps to support continuous improvement of components and processes.
- The challenge is how to facilitate the transmission of critical data in real time.

Digital Response
- GE recently announced a move to capitalize on the fall in the price of sensors which facilitate the monitoring and transmission of performance data from industrial equipment remotely.
- GE is now developing a digital platform with technology partners such as Amazon which will enable it to analyze the vast quantities of data associated with the performance of products such as jet engines (Waters, 2013).
- The move into augmenting a leading position in the manufacture of industrial equipment with the provision of associated data services is another example of GE embracing the opportunities presented by technology.

THE DRIVE FOR SCALABILITY

Stable platforms are key to providing customers, both internal and external, with the confidence that they can rely on a consistent level of service and quality.

Incomplete data, disjointed processes associated with poorly integrated systems and frequent service interruptions for key applications are all examples of technology platform-related issues that have an impact on the consistent level of service and quality provision. This can potentially result in a negative end user experience.

Unstable and inefficient platforms do not scale, requiring additional resource to be expended to keep operations running, and are therefore unable to provide businesses with the strong foundation upon which to build new products and services.

Increasingly, businesses are developing enterprise-wide digital platforms that reuse common processes and focus on core principles, such as a single view of customer data, in order to facilitate scalability.

By developing technology with scalability as a core principle, digital platforms are able to overcome many of the challenges associated with legacy platforms.

FIGURE 12: 7-ELEVEN JAPAN DIGITAL PLATFORM CASE STUDY
CASE STUDY 3:

General Electric uses a digital platform to deliver data services
Background
- The 7-Eleven convenience store chain has grown to over 50,250 stores in over 20 countries, and adds another store to its worldwide operations every 2 hours (Seven-Eleven Japan Co., Ltd., 2013).
- Seven-Eleven Japan (SEJ) is one of the most successful arms of the business, posting 38 years of consecutive sales growth from 1974 to date (Seven-Eleven Japan Co., Ltd., 2013).

Challenge
- An ongoing challenge for retailers is the accurate management of stock. This is even more acute within convenience stores who typically do not have large stock rooms to hold additional product in reserve.
- SEJ needs to understand its stock position on a perpetual basis in order to make sure it has the right products, in the correct quantities, available to customers to avoid losing sales.

> **Digital Response**
> - The digital platform SEJ has developed allows their businesses to process and analyze point-of-sale (POS) data in real time, in order to coordinate the demand and supply of products across the entire supply chain.
> - Through reducing the processing time between sales orders placed and the replenishment of products, SEJ are able to prevent out-of-stock occurrences, which would ultimately result in missed sales. Hand-held terminals used by staff collect information on products and customers which is fed back to head office in real time.
> - Data relating to sales performance, product ranges and weather conditions connects all elements of the supply chain (stores, headquarters and suppliers) (Weill & Ross, 2009).

HOW TO PLAN A DIGITAL PLATFORM

Now that we know what a digital platform is, what the drivers for developing one are and how different businesses are using these platforms to drive business growth and disrupt industries, let us explore some immediate practical steps that can enable businesses to start planning how to develop their digital platform.

UNDERSTAND WHERE THE BUSINESS CURRENTLY IS

If the existing technology platform is in a similar situation to the plate of "cold spaghetti" scenario, then the first step for any company must be to truly understand the current landscape. What applications and hardware are in place, how are they integrated and, perhaps most importantly, what are the current challenges facing the business?

UNDERSTAND WHAT CAN BE REUSED, WHAT CAN BE BUILT UPON AND WHAT MAY NEED TO BE RETIRED

First, it is important to work with the wider business to understand who the customer is, what they want and how current challenges are a barrier to enabling the delivery of a better customer experience. Only then can the enterprise start to think about how it may be possible to reuse existing components of the technology platform, and also identify what is not fit for purpose and therefore should be replaced.

PUT THE DIGITAL PLATFORM IN THE CONTEXT OF WIDER BUSINESS TRANSFORMATION

Whilst a digital platform is a hugely important element of a business transformation, it is only one element of transforming the wider operating model.

Work must also be done to understand the capabilities, both from a technology and non-technology-orientated perspective, roles and structures that will be needed in the future, and this mix should be managed, employing both internal and third-party resource.

Even this may not be enough, as some industries are being disrupted at such a pace that the core business model will need to be re-designed.

Businesses across all industries are recognizing that to survive and hopefully thrive in the digital era, they need to embrace the opportunities new technologies bring, in order to deliver better products and services to customers. A digital platform is a key part of the response, but it should be thought about in the wider context of business transformation.

FIGURE 13: PLANNING A DIGITAL PLATFORM

Where is the business now?	■ What are the current challenges customers face? ■ What applications and software are in place? ■ How are they integrated?
What can be reused and what should be retired?	■ What existing components of technology platforms can be reused and how? ■ What components of existing technology have to be discarded? ■ What do they need to be replaced with?
Is there a bigger question?	■ What are the primary challenges that are facing the existing business model? ■ Is the existing business model going to survive digital disruption?
What capabilities are needed to run the platform?	■ What are the existing capabilities and what capabilities might be needed in the future? ■ What are the skills, roles and structures that will be needed in the future?

KEY TAKEAWAYS:

1. Legacy technology platforms will be a barrier to the delivery of future growth
2. Generating actionable insight from the oceans of data that are available will require new skills and capabilities
3. The digital platform is only one element of the wider transformation agenda. Processes and people are just as important

1.4 THE RISE OF DIGITAL MONEY

DIGITAL MONEY AND THE REALITY OF THE ECONOMIC FUTURE

GLOBAL, SOCIAL AND MOBILE are today's buzzwords in the context of consumer growth. These three realms are considered to be the way forward when it comes to providing cutting-edge, innovative services. More than ever, consumers are becoming empowered by the use of new technologies, and it is these technology-savvy customers that are changing the rules of commerce and shifting the balance of power in their favour when it comes to the relationships they have with brands. When a new product is released, it is likely to first be adopted by consumers who are more open to innovation than others, and more so now as economies grow richer and their populations become more "tech savvy".

Of all the recent creative customer experience offerings, innovation in payments has established a firm foothold with consumers, and enterprises are, therefore, able to reap the rewards:

- The movement of money globally is imperative to all organisations and the ease and simplicity of this movement are key differentiators for true innovators;
- The convergence of the internet and mobile technologies is creating new demands for electronic payments;
- Consumers want the ability to easily pay online, via mobile phone or in social networking/gaming environments; and
- Merchants are looking to payments companies to provide the innovation and leadership needed to keep pace with these rapid developments.

An Elix-IRR paper discussed the rise of mobile payments stemming from African trailblazer M-Pesa, who found a new way to give the "unbanked" access to banking products via mobile technologies. Many global organisations have since played copycat, applying this concept from the developing to the developed world. Organisations such as Visa, MasterCard, Barclays and Starbucks are creating a new wave of innovative thinking by forming alliances with telecoms and technology companies to enhance their offerings, simultaneously blurring the lines between established industries.

PATH OF INNOVATION
GLOBAL SHIFT TOWARDS DIGITAL PAYMENTS

Digital money is driving disruption in channel interaction with

---

[1] An Elix-IRR paper 'M-Africa: Leading the way for the rest of the world' (http://www.elix-irr.com/white-papers/m-africa-leading-way-rest-world

consumers by accelerating the rise of cashless payments and delivering new products to consumers.

In the past 60 years, the payment platform has rapidly evolved from cheque to card, to contactless, to mobile. Payment channels such as PayPal, which were considered "alternative payments" just a few years ago, are now viewed as mainstream (see Figure 15 overleaf). There has been a rise in cashless payments with the rollout of contactless cards and ongoing innovations in retail payments, catering for small denominations. Banking organisations such as Barclays and ABSA have recognised this and introduced contactless payment devices that cater for purchases under the value of £20.

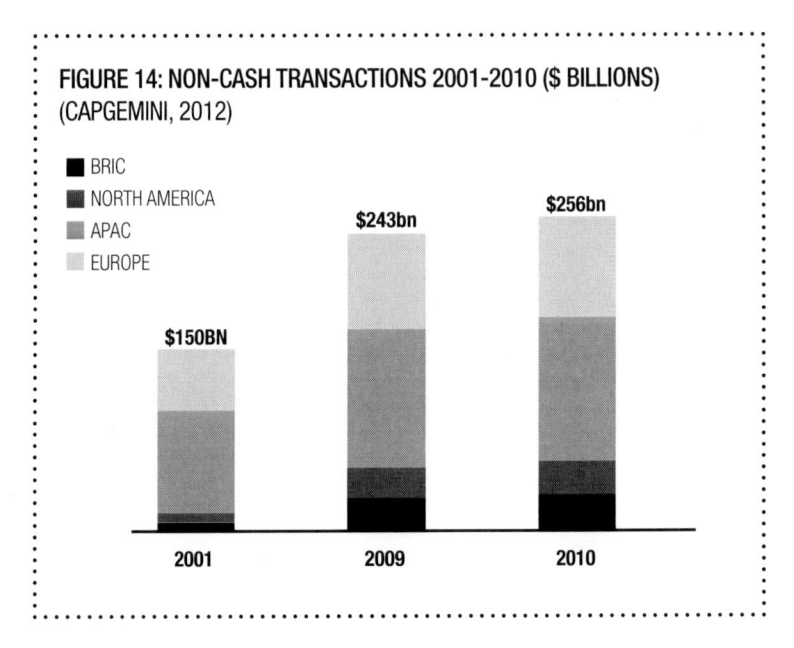

FIGURE 14: NON-CASH TRANSACTIONS 2001-2010 ($ BILLIONS) (CAPGEMINI, 2012)

- BRIC
- NORTH AMERICA
- APAC
- EUROPE

- 2001: $150BN
- 2009: $243bn
- 2010: $256bn

THE RISE OF CASHLESS PAYMENTS

The first contactless smart card in production use for fare payment was the Octopus card, introduced in Hong Kong in 1997 for the territory's mass transit system.

The global volume of non-cash payments has continued to show healthy growth (see Figure 14 above), with the largest gain in volumes occurring in developing markets (average growth for APAC and BRIC over 200% versus Europe and N. America's growth of ~50%) (Elix-IRR analysis).

According to Visa, 60,000 merchant outlets now accept contactless payment in and around London and by the end of 2013 the majority of the capital's transport network will also accept contactless payments (Balaban, 2011).

Research by the World Payments Report shows that the number of payments via mobile devices (m-payments) could grow by 52.7% a year to reach 17 billion in 2013 (Capgemini, 2012).

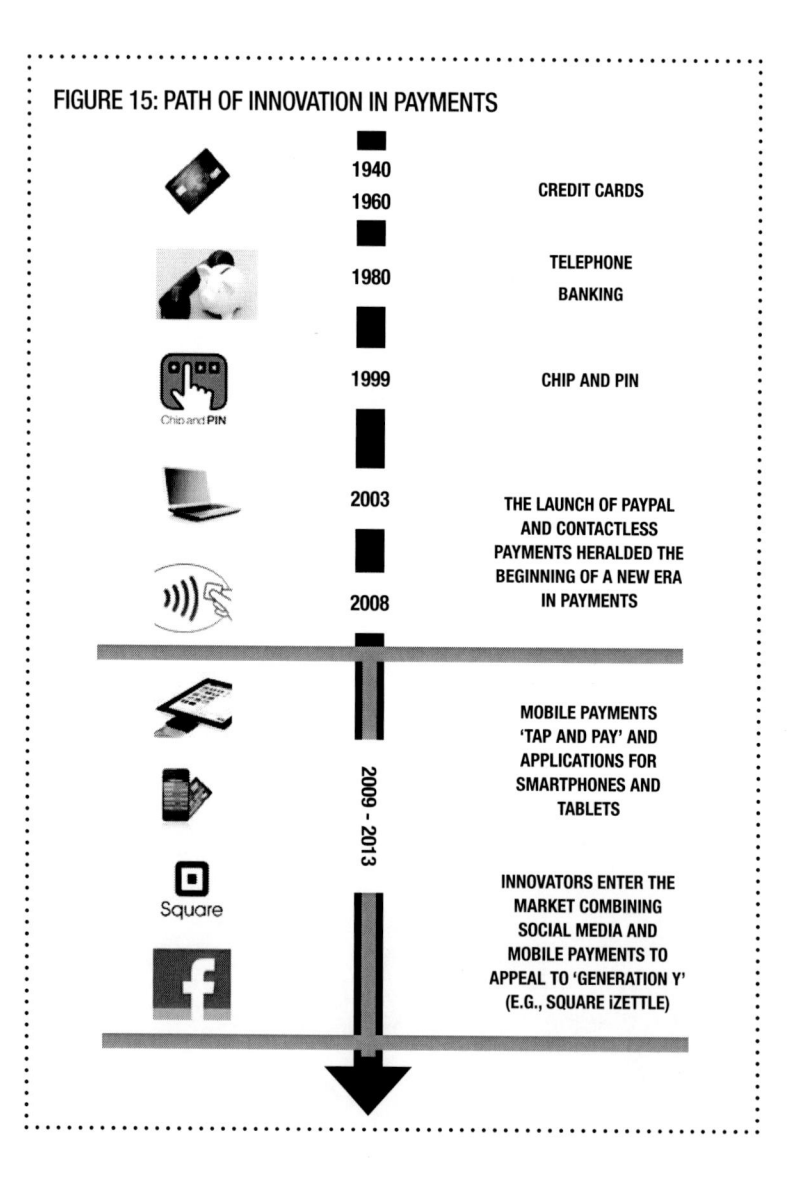

FIGURE 15: PATH OF INNOVATION IN PAYMENTS

1940 – 1960	CREDIT CARDS
1980	TELEPHONE BANKING
1999	CHIP AND PIN
2003	THE LAUNCH OF PAYPAL AND CONTACTLESS PAYMENTS HERALDED THE BEGINNING OF A NEW ERA IN PAYMENTS
2008	
2009 – 2013	MOBILE PAYMENTS 'TAP AND PAY' AND APPLICATIONS FOR SMARTPHONES AND TABLETS
2009 – 2013	INNOVATORS ENTER THE MARKET COMBINING SOCIAL MEDIA AND MOBILE PAYMENTS TO APPEAL TO 'GENERATION Y' (E.G., SQUARE iZETTLE)

DISRUPTIVE COMPANIES BUCKING THE TREND

Innovation leaders have a greater understanding of the needs of their existing markets whilst also being responsive enough to exploit potential new market opportunities and technologies. Such companies will be able to introduce new products and services that will have a direct impact on their ongoing success. Figure 16 below provides a few examples of innovative payments companies, while Figure 17 looks at enterprises that are experimenting with new payment mechanisms.

FIGURE 16: DISRUPTIVE AND INNOVATIVE PAYMENT COMPANIES

Square	- Based in the US, Square is a payment solution that offers a mobile register and a wallet - Square Register serves as a free full point-of-sale system for businesses to accept payments, track inventory and monitor daily reports - Square Wallet is an app that enables customers to buy items directly from their mobile device (Square, Inc., 2013)
iZettle	- This technology is being heralded as the UK and Europe's answer to Square, and allows anyone to take secure card payments via a smartphone or tablet - Launched in the UK exclusively with EE and accepts MasterCard, Visa, American Express and Diners Club (iZettle, 2013)
Ven	- Ven is a currency used to power all exchanges within social network Hub Culture. Members of Hub Culture invite others into the network to buy Ven, and it is available inside Facebook - Its main use is to send payments that can be exchanged at zero cost to anyone with an email address - Used to buy commodities as well as smaller items - The currency is moving into financial trading, markets and funds, and a partnership with Thomson Reuters is delivering Ven pricing data to its data terminals (Ven, 2013)
Bitcoin	- This virtual currency scheme was designed and implemented by Japanese programmer Satoshi Nakamoto in 2009 and is based on a peer-to-peer network similar to file-sharing programme Bit Torrent - Operating on a global level, the currency can be used for virtual transactions, services and real goods, and therefore competes with official currencies like the Euro and US dollar - The scheme maintains a database that lists product and service providers that currently accept Bitcoins (We Use Coins, 2013)

FIGURE 17: EXAMPLES OF TODAY'S ENTERPRISES USING INNOVATIVE PAYMENT MECHANISMS

Starbucks	■ The Seattle-based coffee giant's year-and-a-half-old mobile payment programme may be the largest of any retailer in North America ■ Even before its $25 million investment in San Francisco mobile payments start-up Square, the company had been processing a million mobile phone transactions per week (Flacy, 2011)
First National Bank	■ South Africa's First National Bank (FNB), a division of FirstRand Limited, was named the world's most innovative bank of the year at the 2012 BAI-Finacle Global Banking Innovation Awards ■ The bank's eWallet, a mobile money transfer solution launched in 2009, was also named as a finalist in the Product/Service Innovation category of the competition (First National Bank, 2013)
ICICI Bank	■ India's second-largest bank is leveraging technology to create new platforms for its burgeoning customer base ■ 2011 saw the launch of online banking apps through Facebook that take a lead in connecting social networks with financial services (ICICI Bank, 2013)
Citi	■ N-Wallet by Hana Bank in South Korea and Citibank. Taiwan's N-wallet and mobile payment tools won the Banker/FT innovative banking award in 2013 for innovation and payment respectively ■ HanaBank is the first bank in Asia to offer e-wallet to those without a bank account (Kong, 2012)
Turkcell	■ Turkcell launched a commercial Near Field Communication (NFC) payments platform in Turkey, in collaboration with Yapi Kredi Bank ■ By March 2012, they had attracted over 50,000 active users of their mobile wallet service and over 300,000 mobile subscribers using NFC capable phones (Clark, 2012)

PAYMENTS ARE EVOLVING

The payments world is constantly evolving. So, which of the modern alternative models are likely to disrupt the way in which payments are conducted in the future? And which of the global companies will lead the way?

The world is ever-more connected and the payments sector is helping establish a new culture for creative organisations that are willing to embrace social media, invest in mobile technologies and truly go global.

Customers want their brand interactions to be enabled via the channels they use, such as social and mobile. This applies to everything from the mechanisms they use to pay for purchases to the activities that earn loyalty points.

Today's innovators are embracing disruption and are reaping the rewards by being first to market. As the payments world becomes increasingly disrupted, it will be interesting to see which brands emerge as winners in the battle for control of this space. Figure 18 poses a number of key questions that those competing in this space should be asking.

FIGURE 18: CAPITALIZING ON PAYMENTS INNOVATION – KEY QUESTIONS TO ASK

1. Is the business's current strategy to innovate (be leading edge) or follow (leverage established ideas)?
2. Is the firm "liked" on Facebook, followed on Twitter, linked on LinkedIn? Do the marketing and brand strategy embrace innovative thinking and showcase the latest products and services?
3. Is the business missing out on customer acquisition, retention and development opportunities that the innovative payment platforms can offer?
4. Can it benefit from taking a globally integrated view of how it interacts with customers?
5. Can the organisation form strategic alliances with leading telecoms or offshore technology organisations to leap-frog ahead of its competitors?
6. Does the organisation have the right internal and external capabilities to deliver a successful payment solution?

KEY TAKEAWAYS:

1. The payments landscape is evolving at a dramatic pace
2. Global, social and mobile are all key areas to consider as part of a business' payments strategy
3. Disruption is being driven by new entrants and new technologies

2. DRIVING EFFICIENCY &INSIGHT

CHAPTER OVERVIEW

In this chapter, we consider how retailers can become more efficient by refining operations in the front office through customer returns, and in the back office through more robust and integrated planning. We also discuss an emerging core driver of value for retailers in our section on Big Data.

2.1 THE CUSTOMER RETURNS OPPORTUNITY

Recent estimates of the cost of customer returns to UK retailers are as high as £10 billion annually, with up to 40% of purchases returned in some product categories (McGulloch, 2012). With the growth of multichannel retail, the volume of returns that retailers can expect to handle is only likely to increase. How well a retailer deals with returns not only makes or breaks the customer experience, but also significantly impacts the retailer's bottom line.

This chapter explores the root causes driving customer returns, examines the key challenges facing retailers and discusses the strategic and tactical responses available to turn this growing challenge into an opportunity for retailers to improve their bottom line.

2.2 INTEGRATED BUSINESS PLANNING: AVOIDING "SLASH & BURN" TACTICS IN A GLOBAL DOWNTURN

The existing economic climate is pushing organisations to constantly look for ways to reduce costs, extract efficiencies and execute business objectives with increased agility. With the back office a typical target for cost cutting, what measures can companies implement to ensure a selective and strategic reduction of costs and avoid "slash and burn" tactics?

This chapter focuses on how to develop a coordinated approach to planning in order to enable more strategic decisions regarding where to cut costs and where to invest.

2.3 BIG DATA IN RETAIL

Investing in big data and advanced analytics can be a daunting prospect for retailers, especially in times of reduced margins and fierce competition. In this section, we attempt to define Big Data, how it can be used by retailers to gain a competitive edge, and discuss some of the associated barriers to success from an organisational perspective. We argue that there are a number of unique pre-requisites for retailers to consider before they are ready to transform raw data into actionable insight. Being a data specialist in retail is as much about people and culture as it is resources, tools and technology.

2.1 THE CUSTOMER RETURNS OPPORTUNITY

RETURNS CAN MAKE OR BREAK THE CUSTOMER EXPERIENCE

RECENT ESTIMATES OF the cost of customer returns to UK retailers suggests that the figure could be as high as £10 billion annually (McGulloch, 2012), with up to 40% of purchases returned in some product categories (Morrell, 2013). With the growth of multichannel retail, the volume of returns that retailers can expect to handle is only likely to increase, with the customer trend to "buy, try and return" accelerating.

How well a retailer deals with returns not only makes or breaks the customer experience, but also significantly impacts the retailer's bottom line. If the returns process is handled well, it has the potential to create brand evangelists and contribute to developing the lifetime value of a customer to the business. However, if handled badly, it can destroy a potentially profitable relationship, erode margins and create significant operational challenges.

Despite the positive commercial impact that proactive returns management can deliver, it continues to be a poor relation when compared with the investment that retailers make in support of outbound sales. This is a missed opportunity, considering the more immediate boost to profitability that reducing the volume of returned goods can deliver.

This section explores the root causes driving customer returns, examines the key challenges facing retailers and discusses the strategic and tactical responses available to turn this growing challenge into an opportunity for retailers to improve their bottom line.

ANALYSIS OF CUSTOMER RETURNS (MORRELL, 2013)

- Over 90% of returned stock can be reprocessed and resold
- Processing a return can cost up to three times the price of the initial shipment
- Returned goods can diminish profitability by over 30%
- The cost of returns to some companies can be up to 5% of revenues

WHAT'S DRIVING THE RISE IN CUSTOMER RETURNS?
In this section we consider the main drivers of customer returns.

ELEVATED CUSTOMER EXPECTATIONS
There was a time when returns were rare for non-fault related reasons. However, as customer expectations and their demand for convenience has risen, so too has the propensity to return goods simply because of a post-purchase change of mind.

The "buy, try and return" mentality has been driven by the reduced discretionary time many consumers have to browse and consider options pre-purchase. At the same time, the explosion in the breadth of product ranges has led to consumer uncertainty about whether they have made the right choice.

Furthermore, continued growth in the usage of online and mobile channels, and increasing innovation in returns technology, have made purchasing (and returning) anything, anytime, anywhere a realistic expectation for consumers.

RETAILERS ARE RAISING THE BAR
Increasingly, retailers are offering more lenient and convenient returns policies, with the proliferation of channels through which to return products and more efficient processes making it quicker and easier for customers.

Historically, returning a product involved considerable inconvenience on the part of the customer. The process typically involved a customer driving back to the store where the product was purchased, dealing with a customer services representative to explain the reasons for the return, and then potentially walking away with a credit note. In comparison, today's leading retailers are more likely to operate a "no questions asked" approach in order to satisfy the customer.

This, together with the evolution of supply chain technologies and processes (for example, accepting products bought online as a return in store – known by the acronym BORIS), has raised the benchmark for all retailers. It is now quicker and easier for consumers to return faulty or unwanted goods.

As a result, retailers must balance delivering an outstanding customer experience whilst avoiding becoming an easy target for fraud.

FRAUDULENT ACTIVITY – THE DARK SIDE OF RETURNS
Unfortunately, the rise in returns volumes is also being driven by increased instances of fraud. According to the National Retail Federation (NRF), returns fraud, or "de-shopping", cost American retailers $14.4 billion

in 2011, representing more than a 50% increase on 2009 (Economist, Return to vendor: a dress on loan, 2012).

The spectrum of what constitutes returns fraud is wide, from individuals returning an item that they may have already used, to large-scale organized internet crime, whereby high volumes of stolen goods are refunded. A major challenge for retailers is, therefore, how to identify potentially fraudulent returns.

GROWTH OF INTERNATIONAL RETURNS

The growth of cross-border shopping has led to international returns becoming an area of significant focus for many retailers. As with deliveries, it is relatively straightforward in the EU and many developed countries, but far more complicated outside of these markets.

Within the EU, many retailers that do offer a basic returns service include a generic returns label, and advise the shopper to take items to the post office. Refunds are then arranged according to the specific retailer's policy. Returns from the EU are straightforward as there are no outbound customs duties.

Unfortunately, there are many retailers who choose to leave it up to the shopper to work out their returns route. This is not dissimilar to the domestic market five years ago, and undoubtedly causes customers additional effort and frustration.

Managing the transit of products through customs presents retailers operating internationally with additional challenges. Choosing third-party logistics providers with a global reach is one way to limit the complications of grappling with shipping taxes and customs.

SUPPLIER AGREEMENTS

In the past, retailers have been able to push at least some of the cost of returns back up the supply chain. However, as suppliers increasingly look to protect their own margins, they are introducing volume agreements and caps on the number of returns from retailers in order to limit them. These arrangements are typically based on supplier benchmarks of the rate of returns for their products across the markets in which they operate.

As a result, retailers find themselves in the middle of a squeeze between customers and suppliers as customer return rates increase, whilst suppliers look to limit their own losses by using contractual mechanisms.

ENVIRONMENTAL PRESSURES AND REGULATION

As pressure increases on retailers to monitor the impact of the end-to-end supply chain on the environment, subjects such as energy consumption, emissions levels, and the correct handling and disposal of potentially harmful products and packaging have become important areas of focus.

Regulation such as the Waste Electrical and Electronic Equipment (WEEE) directive has increased the requirement for retailers to monitor how product components are handled through to their end of life.

More stringent reporting requirements and the need for greater supply chain transparency are introducing additional costs for retailers to absorb as part of understanding the true net cost of returned goods.

ALL RETURNS ARE NOT EQUAL
A RETURN RATE OF UP TO 40% IN SOME PRODUCT CATEGORIES

There is a considerable amount of variation in rates of return across different categories of products. Research has highlighted that the spread of returns can vary from 2% to 40% depending on the category (Morrell, 2013). Rates of return are also growing at different speeds. A large survey of consumer electronics noted a 21% increase in the cost of returns, with more than half of the retailers surveyed reporting increases (Douthit, 2012).

Rates of return are influenced by factors such as the channel through which the purchase is made or the time of year it is made. For example, in the shoes category a return rate of one out of every three purchases is common (Millar, 2013), whilst in January retailers can typically expect that up to 40% of clothing and 10% of electrical goods and homewares purchased online will be returned (see Figure 19).

Clearly, retailers who choose to adopt a one-size-fits-all approach for returns will fail to account for the nuances between categories, channels and times.

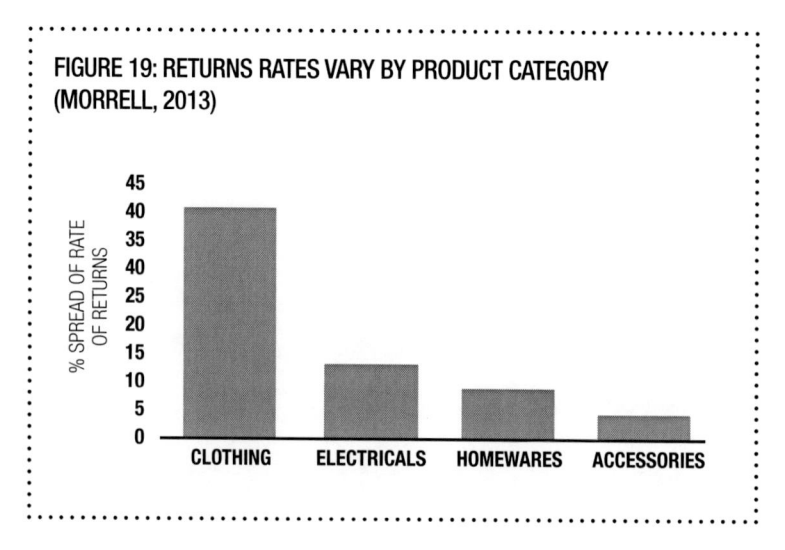

FIGURE 19: RETURNS RATES VARY BY PRODUCT CATEGORY (MORRELL, 2013)

Category	% Spread of Rate of Returns
CLOTHING	40
ELECTRICALS	~13
HOMEWARES	~8
ACCESSORIES	~2

HOW RETAILERS CAN TACKLE RETURNS
ALIGN THE RETURNS STRATEGY TO THE BUSINESS STRATEGY

Retailers should have a returns strategy in place that supports the business' strategy. If a key pillar of the overall retail strategy is to focus on differentiation through excellence in customer service, then a returns policy that minimizes inconvenience on the part of the customer will support this objective. Offering home collection or providing returns labels and reusable packaging are examples of initiatives that can support a customer-focused agenda.

Similarly where multichannel retail is at the heart of the strategy, retailers must put in place the technology and processes to support customer returns through the end-to-end supply chain, and not just view returns as an afterthought.

Leading retailers are adopting innovative approaches through partnerships. For example, John Lewis recently announced its selection of Collect+, which provides its customers with the ability to return online purchases for free through its network of local convenience stores, newsagents and petrol stations (Buter, 2013).

ACTIVELY MANAGE RETURNS

Retailers should look to actively manage returns, so that they become a tool to help maximize profits, rather than a troublesome distraction.

In some cases, a stricter returns policy can actually reduce profits by depressing sales along with returns. Instead, retailers can steer their customers toward the optimal rate of returns without endangering sales by understanding what factors drive returns and adjusting policies and marketing messages accordingly. To do this, retailers need to capture, analyze and report on the reasons for product returns in order to learn and drive improvements into the product, packaging and customer service offered. Data capture and analysis facilitates greater understanding regarding quality or fault issues which need to be addressed with suppliers, or whether the packaging has been inadequate leading to damage in transit.

Tracking and reporting returns data facilitates more informed decision making, and provides evidence to work with the commercial, supply chain, and retail and online teams to make the necessary changes.

Additional areas where data analysis can add value include using customer data to understand if returns are coming from high-value or low-value customers, thus helping to tailor the type of intervention used to protect the most valuable customer relationships. This potentially means segmenting customers to encourage fewer returns by some lower-value customers, and more returns by high-value customers where the net effect of supporting more initial purchases, despite expecting more returns, is an overall increase in final sales per customer.

Leading retailers are starting to implement predictive analytics to support the returns process. The ability to predict whether a certain product category in a certain channel at a certain time has a greater probability of being returned will help in the planning and development of tailored interventions.

VIEW RETURNS AS PART OF THE OVERALL CUSTOMER EXPERIENCE

There will always be some level of returns, so retailers who view the process as an extension of the customer's shopping journey will help to focus attention on the overall objective of better service. Turning a potentially negative experience into a positive one could turn an unhappy customer into a brand evangelist.

THINK ABOUT RETURNS UP-FRONT

Thinking about returns at the initial design stage of a product, rather than at the end of the sales process, can yield benefits for retailers. For example, by considering the packaging requirements at the outset, goods may become resalable far quicker than if there is a requirement to return them to a reprocessing centre.

In addition, buyers should define returns agreements with suppliers as part of their negotiations. All too often a focus on the "top line" without due consideration of the net impact from returns results in slimmer net margins. Therefore, buying teams should ensure that returns processes and commercials are negotiated with suppliers as part of their agreements, and that product pricing reflects the impact of returns. Critically, retailers must also ensure that "supplier agreements" are fully adhered to by staff, in order to prevent unnecessary write-offs and therefore protect cash flow.

PROCESS, GRADE AND SEGREGATE RETURNS

On many occasions returns are unavoidable. Therefore, staff must be encouraged to treat the returned item with as much care as an inbound product, ensuring its speedy progression back through the supply chain, so that the item can be reprocessed and put back on the shelf for resale as quickly as possible.

OFFER AN ALTERNATIVE

Providing the convenience to customers to exchange an unwanted product in store and have immediate access to an alternative is far more likely to result in an "exchange", as opposed to online where they are most likely to demand a refund.

FRAUD PREVENTION

Retailers can reduce fraudulent returns by introducing a process to identify them, for example via the introduction of a standard process for quality assurance for returned products, to ensure that if the item is not faulty, it is resalable.

PARTNER STRATEGICALLY

In many cases, the limitation of effective returns management has been a lack of scale and volume. Therefore, companies are increasingly using third parties to consolidate and process returns cost-effectively to customers, and maximize recovery value.

CONCLUSION: THE CUSTOMER RETURNS OPPORTUNITY

- Customer returns are an increasingly important area to actively manage as pressure on margins and consumer expectations increases;
- Adopting a one-size-fits-all approach across all categories will fail to account for the multiple challenges the management of customer returns poses;
- Retailers need to think carefully about both their overall returns strategy and the tactical interventions at their disposal;
- Active management of returns can deliver better margins and increase customer satisfaction; and
- Customer returns are inevitable – the challenge will always exist, and retailers should use this experience as an opportunity to delight, rather than frustrate, the customer.

KEY TAKEAWAYS:

1. Returns are a critical part of the customer experience
2. Customers increasingly expect to be able to return goods anywhere and at any time
3. Active management of returns can deliver better margins and increase customer satisfaction

2.2 INTEGRATED BUSINESS PLANNING

AVOIDING "SLASH AND BURN" TACTICS IN A GLOBAL DOWNTURN

RECESSION HAS FORCED most industries to engage in sustained periods of cost cutting – however, many companies have not done this strategically, but have rather engaged in tactical cost control.

The existing economic climate is pushing organisations to constantly look for ways to reduce costs, extract efficiencies and execute on business objectives with increased agility. One of the most common ways to do this is still to implement operating efficiencies and cut costs across back office functions (e.g., HR, IT, Finance), especially staff costs and discretionary projects (e.g., in IT). However, companies that use short-term cost-cutting tactics during a recession often find that this affects their long-term growth. For example:

- Many banks such as UBS, Deutsche Bank and Credit Suisse are now on their second round of headcount reductions since 2009. Previous redundancy exercises were not properly structured, the headcount rapidly increased again, cost reduction was not sustainable, and the prolonged recession has led to them having to pull on the same lever once more.
- BT cut their graduate programme in 2009 to save costs, but in doing so potentially restricted their access to future talent (Cooper, 2009).
- Lehman Brothers had the lowest cost/income ratio on Wall Street when it declared bankruptcy – despite being very efficient from a cost perspective, a lack of focus on core capabilities in other areas proved to be very costly.

A 2010 Harvard Business Review study into which companies prospered post-recession argued that it was not those that conducted "slash and burn" tactics to reduce costs that survived, but those that were selective in cost cutting and maintained strategic investments (Gulati, Nohria, & Wohlgezogen, 2010). A small proportion of companies studied – 9% of the sample – flourished after a slowdown, doing better on key financial measures than they had before the crisis, and outperforming rivals in their industry by at least 10% in terms of sales and profits growth. The study showed that these were the companies that reduced costs selectively by focusing more on operational efficiency than their rivals, even as they invested in marketing, R&D and other assets.

With the back office being a typical target for cost cutting, what measures can companies implement to ensure a selective and strategic reduction of costs?

This chapter focuses on an integrated and coordinated approach to planning to facilitate more strategic decisions on where to cut costs and where to continue to invest in capabilities.

MOST ORGANISATIONS LACK A COHERENT APPROACH TO PLANNING

Planning effectively and having access to the right information at the right time allows organisations to balance investment in key activities with sustainable cost reduction. Research shows that almost 70% of organisations are in need of substantial improvement in their planning effectiveness and that the majority have difficulty coordinating plans across the organisation and effectively assessing the impact of major changes to existing plans (Ventana Research, 2010).

Given the increasingly challenging and fast-paced environment organisations operate in, an annual corporate budget combined with individual departments' forecasts is no longer adequate to ensure an organisation's ability to survive and be competitive in the marketplace.

There are tangible benefits to having plans linked together. Research shows that 85% of respondents whose companies provide all the information they need to understand the impact of proposed trade-offs say their plans are accurate; for those who reported that they were unable to measure the impacts of the trade-offs, only 40% said their plans are accurate (Ventana Research, 2010) (see Figure 20 for more details). So, how can organisations coordinate and improve the accuracy of various plans across the organisation?

Organisations today engage in many forward-looking activities. The implementation of a robust Integrated Business Planning process, managed by a central coordinating function, has proven to be effective in driving alignment across an organisation's forecasting and planning activities in a way that supports the achievement of strategic objectives.

COORDINATING ACTIVITIES ACROSS THE BACK OFFICE

A central coordinating function is vital to embedding a robust integrated business planning process in an organisation.

Different businesses have different requirements when it comes to responding to changes and challenges in their environment, but in all cases transformation across functions can be made more successful (quicker, larger, better) if managed centrally.

Historically, back office functions such as IT, Finance and HR have developed their own strategies and followed their own improvement

FIGURE 20: INTEGRATED PLANNING: WHAT BUSINESSES SAY (VENTANA RESEARCH, 2010)

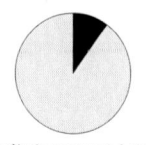

< 10% of business managers & executives surveyed said they had all the information necessary to accurately measure the impact of potential trade-offs within their part of the organisation

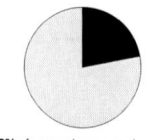

< 22% of companies surveyed are able to do a complete revision to their annual financial plan in response to major charges

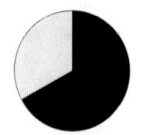

67% of organisations surveyed need to improve the effectiveness of their planning process significantly

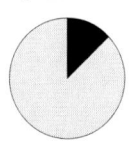

Only 13% of organisations surveyed said they explored the implications of a comprehensive set of business scenarios at the company level

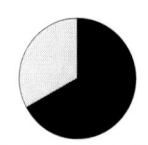

67% of participants surveyed said that a better understanding of the market trends would improve the accuracy of their forecasting process

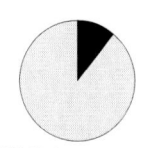

Only 11% of business managers and executives said there was sufficient coordination of plans across their organisation

and transformation journeys. Over the last ten years, however, the implementation of a standardized Operating Model across back office functions, together with the integration and alignment of back office strategies and plans, has been a successful way to extract value and efficiencies. Bringing the back office together under one organisational and governance structure in a Central Office Function (COF) can support this transformation. This function is typically responsible for:

- Better managing strategy and business architecture across the back office;
- Better leveraging existing capabilities where possible; and
- Coordinating implementation planning across the back office functions in an integrated way – the COF provides central coordination of planning and execution of the plan.

THE COF AND INTEGRATED BUSINESS PLANNING

Typically, the Integrated Business Planning process across an organisation's back office functions is driven by the COF. Integrated Business Planning aims to drive internal alignment in an organisation's strategies and plans, enhancing its ability to effectively deliver on its strategic objectives and to respond to changes in the environment. It advocates a cyclical and systemic approach to planning and is a critical step in the strategic planning process, facilitating the identification of strategic initiatives, enabling their prioritization and driving alignment across the business.

The strategic planning process in any organisation is inherently iterative since companies' strategies are constantly being reviewed and re-assessed based on internal and external changes. Having a robust Integrated Business Planning process in place helps to ensure that companies are not "caught out" when such changes occur. Other functions of the COF are shown in Figure 21 below.

FIGURE 21: OVERVIEW OF ADDITIONAL CAPABILITIES/SERVICES THAT CAN BE DELIVERED BY A CENTRAL OFFICE FUNCTION

SERVICE FRAMEWORK	TARGET OPERATING MODELS	PROJECT IMPLEMENTATION	POLICIES	LIMITS OF AUTHORITY
SOURCING STRATEGY	**INTEGRATED BUSINESS PLANNING**	BUSINESS MANAGEMENT	EXECUTIVE REPORTING	IMPLEMENTATION PLANNING
NEW BUSINESS DEVELOPMENT	DATA MANAGEMENT & GOVERNANCE	COST CONTROL	COMMUNICATIONS	CORPORATE POLICY/MARKET INITIATIVES

DELIVERING THE BUSINESS STRATEGY

When changes in the economic environment take place, companies need to respond quickly and effectively, while ensuring that any measures that are implemented do not adversely impact the achievement of the company's long-term strategy and objectives.

In this respect, the implementation of a robust Integrated Business Planning process supports organisations in ensuring their "forward-looking" initiatives are aligned to the overall business strategy, resources are allocated correctly and existing capabilities are leveraged across the organisation. Integrated Business Planning also facilitates other key planning and management processes such as strategy development and communication, financial planning and reporting (including the budgeting process) and performance management. Integrated Business

Planning allows organisations to identify key capabilities that need to be maintained or invested in and to divest non-core/non-strategic activity as opposed to "spreading the pain" across the organisation. Centralized, integrated planning facilitates a holistic view, rather than the typical default process of allocating a portion of required cost savings evenly across budgets.

WHAT DOES AN EFFECTIVE INTEGRATED BUSINESS PLANNING PROCESS LOOK LIKE?

An effective Integrated Business Planning process drives alignment across back office functions and helps to ensure that initiatives being undertaken by the back office effectively support the execution of front office objectives. It also facilitates the timely communication of strategic decisions, imposes critical financial planning guidelines and provides consistent and reliable planning tools across the organisation. When properly implemented, an Integrated Business Planning process enables an organisation to respond to changes rapidly and effectively, and to make trade-offs that do not adversely impact long-term strategy.

HAVING THE APPROPRIATE IT PLATFORMS IN PLACE IS CRITICAL

An Integrated Business Planning process aims to drive alignment across an organisation and support an agile and effective decision-making process. This is rendered almost impossible, or at least slowed down considerably, if the appropriate IT platforms are not implemented in order to facilitate timely access to accurate and up-to-date information. Research has shown that organisations that have access to good quality data, use the right tools, and can easily integrate data from multiple systems frequently tend to develop more accurate plans.

CONCLUSIONS

Companies that embed Integrated Business Planning in their culture will be best positioned to weather recessions and position themselves for future growth.

In a challenging economic climate that pushes organisations to constantly look for ways to reduce costs and extract efficiencies, companies that use short-term cost-cutting tactics could find that this affects their long-term growth trajectories.

Planning effectively and having access to the right information at the right time can allow organisations to balance investment in key activities with sustainable cost reduction. A central coordinating function is a vital component in order to embed a robust integrated business planning process within an organisation, and can be used to drive the

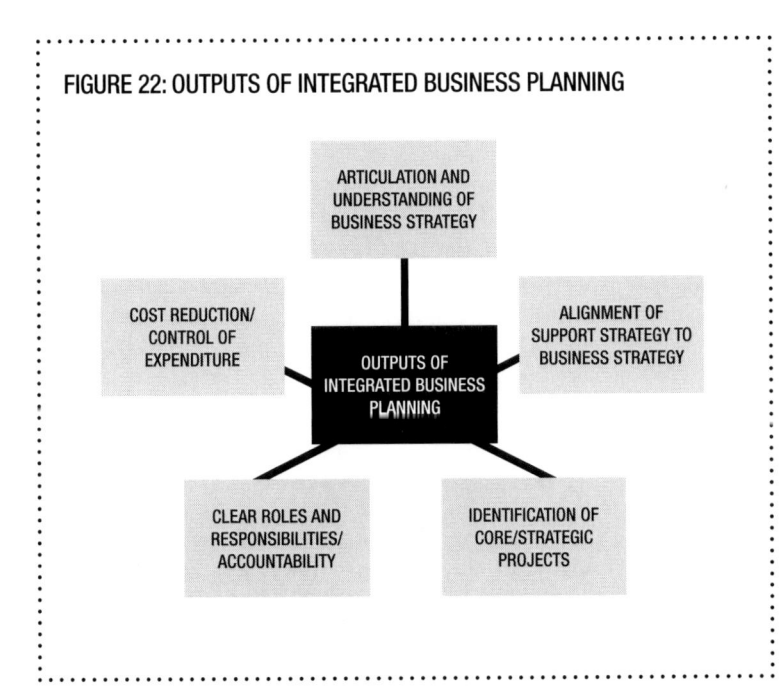

FIGURE 22: OUTPUTS OF INTEGRATED BUSINESS PLANNING

OUTPUTS OF INTEGRATED BUSINESS PLANNING:
- ARTICULATION AND UNDERSTANDING OF BUSINESS STRATEGY
- ALIGNMENT OF SUPPORT STRATEGY TO BUSINESS STRATEGY
- IDENTIFICATION OF CORE/STRATEGIC PROJECTS
- CLEAR ROLES AND RESPONSIBILITIES/ACCOUNTABILITY
- COST REDUCTION/CONTROL OF EXPENDITURE

implementation of a consistent and robust process across the back office.

Integrated Business Planning allows companies to balance investment in key activities with sustainable cost reduction and to take an organisation-wide approach to prioritization rather than just "spreading the pain".

Today, more than ever, it is crucial for companies to be able to respond quickly and effectively to change, ensuring that any measures that are implemented do not adversely impact the achievement of the company's long-term strategy and objectives. Effective planning is the key.

KEY TAKEAWAYS:

1. Short term "slash and burn" approaches to cost cutting can stifle long-term growth
2. Integrated planning via a central coordinating function can help to support selective and strategic cost reduction
3. Establishing a Central Office Function (COF) across back office functions can provide timely access to information to support decision making

2.3 BIG DATA IN RETAIL

THE CONCEPTS OF BIG DATA and Advanced Analytics can be daunting for retailers, especially when margins are under pressure and competition is fierce. In this chapter, we define Big Data, discuss how it can be used by retailers to gain a competitive edge, and cover some of the associated organisational barriers to success that may exist. We argue that there are a number of pre-requisites that retailers should have in place in order to transform raw data into real value-added insight. Being a data specialist in retail is as much about understanding organisations, people and culture as it is about having access to resources, tools and technology.

WHAT IS BIG DATA?

Big Data is an increasingly common term used across industries, including retail. The rapid growth in accessibility to transactional, consumer and performance data is fuelling a paradigm shift in the way retailers do business. For the purpose of this chapter we define Big Data as very large data sets of structured and/or unstructured data. This is data that is extremely large in terms of volume, is streamed at a high velocity and exists in a multitude of formats (Laney, 2001).

In a world of rapidly advancing technology and economic pressures, consumers are becoming savvy and confident; they are demanding more and more transparency from retailers in order to compare and contrast products and prices as they make decisions. As a result of this, tighter margins are in turn driving the need to gain a competitive edge through Big Data initiatives.

Big Data is much more than a huge dataset and access to cutting-edge analytics tools; it is a philosophy that will separate the winners from the losers in the battle for retail supremacy. The growth in its importance is the latest evolution of the role data has played through the history of competitive retail.

THE HISTORY OF DATA IN RETAIL

Before we discuss the opportunity Big Data presents, we begin with a short reminder of the role data has played in retail.

IN THE BEGINNING

Data in retail has historically been used for a sole purpose: stock control. Prior to the automation of global supply chains, all retailers collected data about the products they sold to ensure sufficient stock for the next sale. Before the ubiquity of barcodes and intelligent retail systems, a

FIGURE 23: THE BIG DATA VICIOUS CYCLE

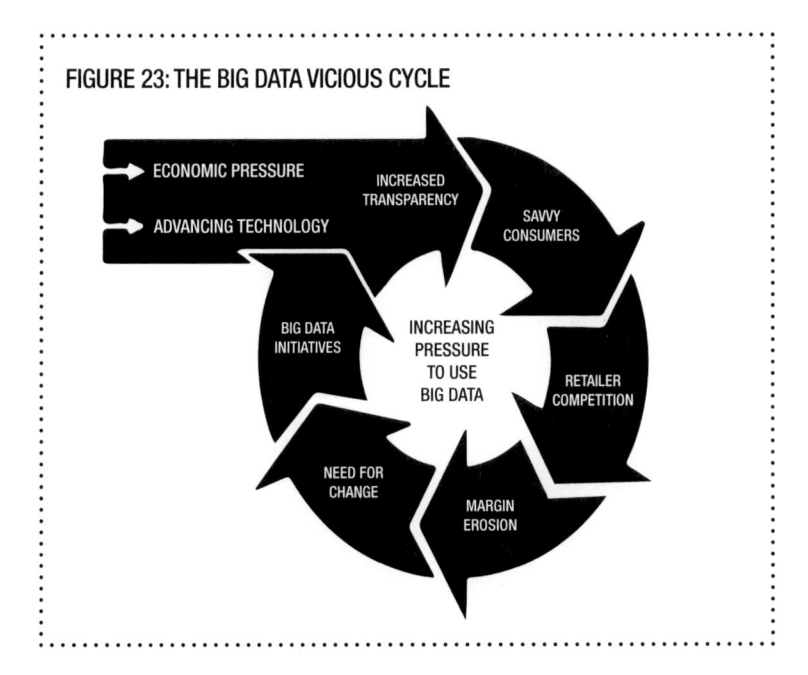

- ECONOMIC PRESSURE
- ADVANCING TECHNOLOGY
- INCREASED TRANSPARENCY
- SAVVY CONSUMERS
- RETAILER COMPETITION
- MARGIN EROSION
- NEED FOR CHANGE
- BIG DATA INITIATIVES
- INCREASING PRESSURE TO USE BIG DATA

corner-shop owner would keep a handwritten ledger detailing sales to customers and purchases of wholesale goods to enable him to know when to restock.

EPOS AND BARCODES

As shops began to roll out barcodes and electronic point-of-sale (ePOS) technologies, data began to be collected and aggregated automatically. This data was then used to help automate the stock-keeping process. Initially, the focus was on improving the availability of stock, but retailers could now focus on ensuring that the right amount of stock was available. However, always having stock available to sell is not necessarily an advantageous strategy in retail, as stock equates to cash, and static stock is a risk to cash flow.

The analysis of data remained relatively simple, and focused on the volume movements of products. Customers' individual spending habits were still opaque, creating a large opportunity for any organisation enterprising enough to harness the power of customer data analytics.

THE INTRODUCTION OF LOYALTY SCHEMES

The introduction of loyalty cards, and perhaps most famously the Tesco Clubcard (in partnership with dunnhumby, whom they subsequently purchased), opened the door to a rich new seam of data linked to consumer behaviour rather than only product information. In exchange for offering the customer rewards in the form of points, the Clubcard enabled Tesco to track and understand the spending habits of their customers. This precipitated a huge shift in the way that retailers were able to manage their data.

- It created the ability to inform range and store options based on extrapolating insight into consumer behaviour;
- Stores and other channels could manage promotions more effectively by understanding the spending habits of local consumers; and
- Promotions could be tailored to the individual, e.g., coupons and other mechanics.

THE INTERNET

The internet created another opportunity to exploit a wealth of data previously unavailable to retailers, allowing them to understand even more about the consumer journey and in response create more intuitive and personalized shopping experiences. As an example, consumers can now personalize stores to ensure that they are only seeing products they are likely to purchase – the ultimate in bespoke product ranging.

Advanced data collection and manipulation software has also helped to create the ubiquitous "personal recommendation", used to great effect by Amazon. Personalized recommendations and offers can now be sent out in great volume over email to customers based on analysis of their spending behaviour. An area of current growth is mobile marketing, which combines technologies such as Geographic Positioning System (GPS) technology with consumer profiles to target customers with specific offers, even in some instances to those who are near the stores of their competitors.

Harnessing the power of data has become a critical part of retail strategy. However, whilst some have enthusiastically embraced its potential, many retailers remain to be convinced of the benefits.

CAPITALIZING ON THE OPPORTUNITY

BARRIERS TO SUCCESS

Inevitably, as is often the case with new technology-enabled paradigms, retailers must overcome a number of barriers in order to capitalize on the opportunity afforded by the innovation.

- **DELAYED RETURN ON INVESTMENT (ROI)** – with constant pressure to maintain a competitive edge, it can appear counterintuitive for any retailer – new or established – to make the large investments in

Big Data initiatives when it will take time to demonstrate a material return.
- **CHALLENGE OF DEMONSTRATING MEASURABLE IMPACT** – Big Data is an enabling function for retailers, and therefore can make a significant impact on the ability to market, form strategy, control inventories and react quickly to trends. However, precisely because it enables these processes, it may be hard to quantify the precise role that Big Data contributes without conducting detailed assessments.
- **COMMUNICATION** – there are a vast array of tools and technologies now available on the market, coupled with a rapidly expanding vocabulary. Making sense of Big Data and being fluent enough to communicate with colleagues is a task in itself that requires an investment of time and effort.
- **INERTIA** – some retailers are intrinsically uncomfortable with moving to a data-driven world. Investing heavily in a scientific approach can go against the grain for traditionalists who might prize intuition and gut-feel over technology-enabled logic.
- **LACK OF CAPABILITY** – even for those who are open to fresh ideas and approaches, it can be a daunting task to select the appropriate tools and methodologies, find the right people and gain sufficient buy-in from decision makers. The capability often requires a new set of skills, experience and understanding of the language of data, and retailers must decide whether to build up the capability internally or select a partner from the increasing array of third-party suppliers.
- **PURPOSE** – hype has resulted in some retailers kicking-off Big Data initiatives without first properly defining the strategic objectives for the investment. The result has, in many cases, been a difficult early journey; a failure to first answer the question of why the initiative is needed has led to directionless programmes and projects. In such scenarios retailers may find their initial investments somewhat wasted, therefore reducing any future appetite to venture into the world of Big Data.
- **INADEQUATE PREPARATION** – some retailers have also suffered from data overload, having launched into Big Data initiatives without first establishing the necessary infrastructure to store and exploit it. Some have found themselves unable to process the vast quantities of data collected, and have had to solve the problem at significant extra cost. Adequate planning and preparation is therefore critical.

TAKING A LEAP OF FAITH

In reality, there is a world of opportunity in exploiting data. The key is being prepared to invest adequate time in planning and understanding the transformation effort required, what to invest in, how much to invest and when.

The implementation of a data programme does not have to follow a strict methodology. Nonetheless, there are some general guidelines that should be followed. A clear data strategy should be formulated up-front, based on measurable return on investment and rigorous scenario testing. Opportunities should be researched and prioritized.

Figure 24 describes a selection of examples where Big Data has been deployed in retail, categorized into three focus areas: customers, products and organisation. These opportunities can be organized and prioritized by teams that understand the costs and benefits of each in the context of the business, and who understand how to capitalize on the increasing amounts of data available in each area.

FIGURE 24: EXAMPLES OF USE OF BIG DATA (ELIX-IRR ANALYSIS)

AREA	BASIC	STRETCH	AMBITIOUS
Product	**Stock control / movement** - Software to facilitate forecasting of sales in real time - Example: **McDonalds**	**Assortment planning** - Use of software to reduce number of SKUs - Example: **Aldi; Costco**	**Real-time promotions** - Scannable coupons if you "check in" store via Foursquare - Example: **Walgreens**
Organisation	**Regional variations** - Analytics used to vary store range by region (e.g., ethnic foods) - Example: **Tesco**	**Optimizing store layout** - Combined footfall with sales density data to display higher margin products accordingly - Example: **American Apparel**	**Predicting behaviour** - Online banking sites that track loan data with help to transfer funds, etc. - Example: **Lloyds**
Customer	**Personalized offers** - Strong personalized offering, in step with strength of overall brand - Example: **John Lewis**	**Customer value-based pricing** - Price realization, backed up by analytics, strengthening buyers - Example: **M&S**	**Targeted marketing** - Exclude certain geographical areas from online marketing due to low return on investment - Example: **Fairy tale Brownies**

ASSESSING BIG DATA CAPABILITY
MEASURES OF CAPABILITY
The strength of a retailers' capability in this field is arguably a function of money and culture, and can be measured across six "asset" categories. Three of these can be bought and are obtainable by retailers with the capacity to make large investments in people (technical capability), processes (methodologies and approaches) and technology (analytical tools).

The other three represent softer capabilities, such as changes to an organisation's culture, customer perceptions, or market presence, and are difficult for small and agile retailers, let alone long-established high-street retailers.

The balance of financial and cultural flexibility summarizes the struggle between high-street and online retailers, as demonstrated by the four types of organisation mapped in Figure 25 overleaf (where 1 indicates "likely weakness" and 5 "likely strength").

THE FUTURE FOR BIG DATA
The capability assessment model provides a general summary of some of the challenges that different types of retailers face. The fact is, there is no tried and tested formula for success in translating Big Data into business value.

For a number of retailers, the high street continues to present opportunities. There is certainly room at both ends of the value spectrum, for large luxury retailers like Apple, as well as for retailers like Poundland and IKEA who are currently unable to find enough sites in the UK to meet demand.

In addition to the opportunities to fill niches, trends are highly variable by both product and geography. It is hard to imagine the vast majority of food or clothing being bought online. However, for books, music and electronics, it is a different story (see Figure 26 overleaf).

The UK is increasing its share of online sales more rapidly than any other country (Figure 27 overleaf). There are clearly opportunities to diversify brands and shift locations, but these opportunities are hard to predict and are a rare commodity.

Retailers have made significant investments in ERP, CRM and other sales force automation systems to manage their businesses more efficiently. All of these systems provide a great deal of data, and it is how this data is used that will determine the winners and losers over the coming years within the retail industry.

The factors that make some retailers reluctant to embrace Big Data can be mitigated by adopting a robust and carefully planned approach

FIGURE 25: BIG DATA CAPABILITY ASSESSMENT TOOL FOR MAINSTREAM RETAILERS

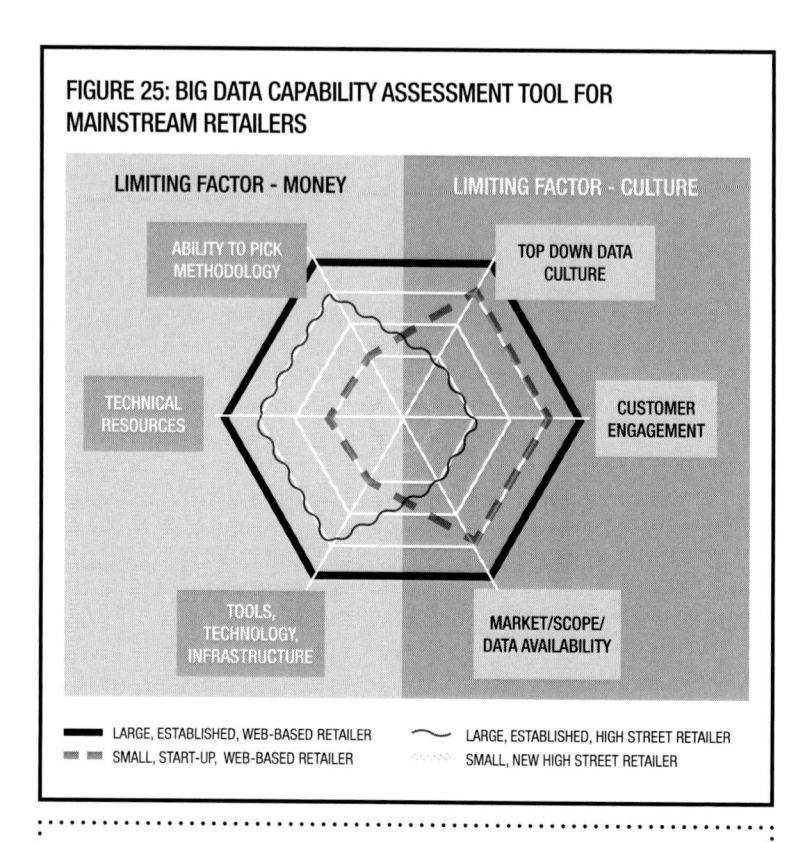

LIMITING FACTOR - MONEY
LIMITING FACTOR - CULTURE

- ABILITY TO PICK METHODOLOGY
- TOP DOWN DATA CULTURE
- TECHNICAL RESOURCES
- CUSTOMER ENGAGEMENT
- TOOLS, TECHNOLOGY, INFRASTRUCTURE
- MARKET/SCOPE/ DATA AVAILABILITY

— LARGE, ESTABLISHED, WEB-BASED RETAILER
∿ LARGE, ESTABLISHED, HIGH STREET RETAILER
▪ ▪ SMALL, START-UP, WEB-BASED RETAILER
⋯ SMALL, NEW HIGH STREET RETAILER

FIGURE 26: ONLINE SALES FORECAST AS A PERCENTAGE OF TOTAL SALES (MCRAE, 2013)

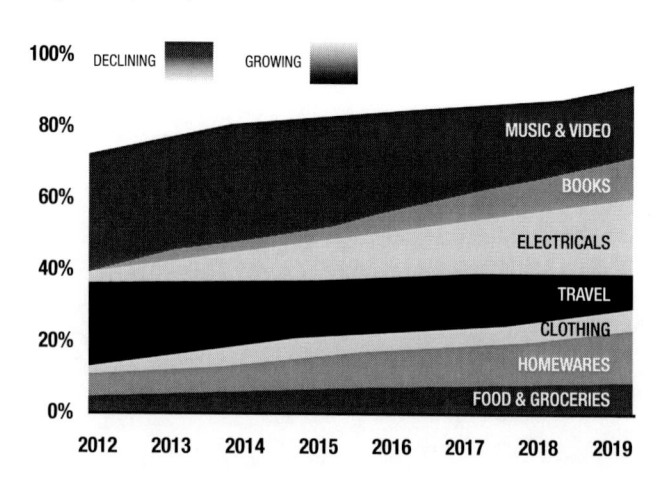

DECLINING   GROWING

- MUSIC & VIDEO
- BOOKS
- ELECTRICALS
- TRAVEL
- CLOTHING
- HOMEWARES
- FOOD & GROCERIES

2012 2013 2014 2015 2016 2017 2018 2019

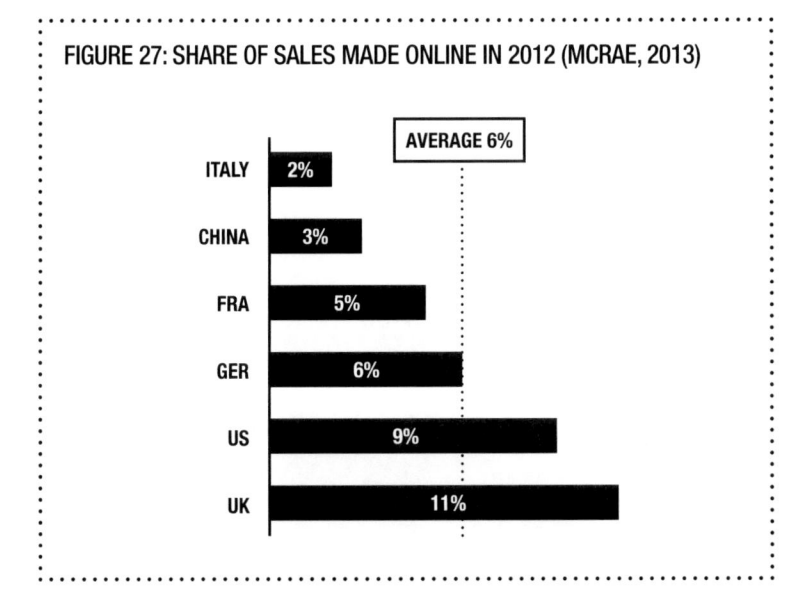

FIGURE 27: SHARE OF SALES MADE ONLINE IN 2012 (MCRAE, 2013)

ITALY	2%
CHINA	3%
FRA	5%
GER	6%
US	9%
UK	11%

AVERAGE 6%

that takes into consideration the retailer's strategy. There is no one-size-fits-all approach. Big Data remains relatively new territory, and few companies have to date developed the internal capability and capacity to fully exploit its potential. However, the price of choosing to do nothing is to potentially risk losing market share and competitive positioning as more and more retailers opt to exploit the power of their data.

Big Data is relevant and important to both "bricks-and-mortar" retailers and online players. The increasing share of the consumer's wallet spent online means that organisations that target consumers most effectively will continue to prosper regardless of whether they have a thousand high-street locations or a single online presence. Embracing evolution is always daunting but necessary to progress.

KEY TAKEAWAYS:

1. The ability to generate insight from the analysis of large and complex datasets is emerging as a key competitive differentiator for retailers
2. However, Big Data initiatives should not be implemented on a reactionary or "me-too" basis
3. A clear data strategy needs to consider the return on investment and involve rigorous testing early on to ensure measurable payback

3.
ORGANIZING FOR SUCCESS

CHAPTER OVERVIEW

In this chapter, we examine how retailers can organize to be better prepared for the challenges they are facing. We discuss the key components for delivering successful business transformations, how adopting a service-based mind-set can help to improve operational efficiency and the key steps involved in designing a practical and achievable Target Operating Model (TOM).

3.1 MAKING BUSINESS TRANSFORMATION A SUCCESS FOR YOUR ORGANISATION

There is increasing pressure on businesses to adapt and structure themselves in a way that allows them to realize greater efficiencies, consolidate their position and take advantage of anticipated market trends. Yet senior leadership are continually faced with the challenge of why the delivery of planned benefits of transformation initiatives rarely materializes.

This chapter seeks to explain why "transformation" initiatives often fail and addresses what retailers can do to get it right.

3.2 ORGANIZATIONAL EXCELLENCE THROUGH SERVICE MANAGEMENT

What common practices can firms learn from to achieve organisational excellence?

In this chapter, we describe how adopting a service mind-set can help an organisation achieve operational efficiency and deliver improved operating margins. We discuss how the implementation of a formalized Service Management Framework is a key element for achieving organisational excellence and for driving a culture of continuous improvement and innovation.

3.3 REMOVING THE "T" FROM YOUR TOM

Many organisations are examining their operating model as a way to cut costs and realize efficiencies. This chapter focuses on how to design a TOM that meets business needs and actually is implemented – and hence is no longer a Target.

The chapter provides practical insight for operating model design, developed from our experience of designing operating models for a wide variety of major enterprises. This insight is structured around our proven TOM design methodology.

3.1 MAKING BUSINESS TRANSFORMATION A SUCCESS

INTRODUCTION
BUSINESS TRANSFORMATION: A REALITY FOR BUSINESSES TODAY

THE PACE OF CHANGE in retail has meant that there is increasing pressure on businesses to adapt and re-structure themselves in order to realize greater efficiencies and respond to emerging market trends. Mergers and acquisitions, divestures, outsourcing/offshoring, company-wide IT initiatives, cross-functional improvement programmes and the restructuring of existing functions are all examples of "transformation" initiatives that represent retailers' intent to address the challenges they face in today's increasingly global competitive environment.

In fact, a recent study by Capgemini indicates that the need to respond to industry challenges – such as increased competition from overseas and domestic competitors, industry consolidation, changing consumer preferences and regulatory/policy change – is the main driver behind business transformation (see Figure 28).

Consider the following example. In the 1990s, a company that manufactured computers and operated an alternative platform was in dire straits. It had experienced decreasing profit levels, and was losing the already relatively small market share it had. Analysts waited for what was viewed as its inevitable collapse. Fast forward to 2012, and the same company (Apple) has achieved the highest market capitalization of any company through a phenomenal transformation into one of the leading digital businesses (Guglielmo, 2012).

At the opposite end of the spectrum, consider a company viewed as one of the pioneers of analogue technology, which was once the number-one photography-related brand. Twenty years ago, revenues peaked at $16 billion and the workforce numbered over 130,000. Roll forward to January 2012 when Eastman Kodak filed for bankruptcy (McCarthy, 2012).

Two examples: one is a testament to the idea that, with the right approach, successful business transformations can take place; the other is a stark reminder that failure to successfully adapt to change will have disastrous consequences.

This chapter discusses why "business transformation" initiatives often fail, and what retailers can do to "get it right", so that instead of an Achilles heel, managing and delivering complex business transformation becomes a core competence.

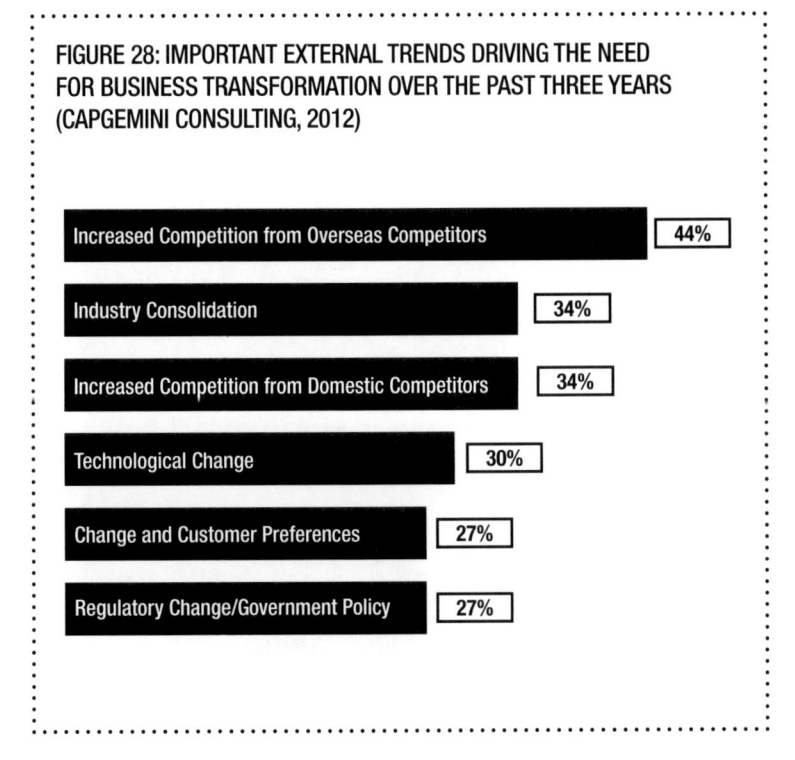

FIGURE 28: IMPORTANT EXTERNAL TRENDS DRIVING THE NEED FOR BUSINESS TRANSFORMATION OVER THE PAST THREE YEARS (CAPGEMINI CONSULTING, 2012)

Trend	Percentage
Increased Competition from Overseas Competitors	44%
Industry Consolidation	34%
Increased Competition from Domestic Competitors	34%
Technological Change	30%
Change and Customer Preferences	27%
Regulatory Change/Government Policy	27%

WHY DO TRANSFORMATION PROGRAMMES FAIL?
1. FAILURE TO ADOPT THE RIGHT STRATEGY

The bankruptcy of Eastman Kodak was not an overnight surprise. Indeed, it was common knowledge that the company had been struggling for almost a decade. Why then was the company unable to change? The lessons learnt from Kodak are something that all organisations should heed.

Kodak was unable to successfully adapt to the pace of the technological change brought about by digitization, with competition from new entrants with associated lower cost structures eroding Kodak's leadership position. While a succession of CEOs planned for Kodak to compete in the digital market, they were unable to find and implement a strategy to help them recover the lost revenues previously earned from their "cash cow" business (silver halide film). Digital was not seen as a threat to the core businesses, as evidenced by its status as a separate operation removed from the mainstream business.

Organisations need to ensure that any strategy openly addresses the reality of the challenges a business, and in many cases an industry, faces.

They should be prepared to adapt/change that strategy in the face of new opportunities and threats.

2. FAILURE TO EXECUTE

The ability to execute a strategy is critical to the success or failure of transformation initiatives. A recent study (see Figure 29) shows that 38% of respondents felt that "implementation" was the stage where projects most often succumbed to failure. Other critical stages identified include "communication of objectives" (13%) and "formulation of strategy and transformation objectives" (12%). Related to implementation is the requirement to undertake adequate planning. Poor planning, and implicitly a lack of risk analysis and mitigation, will often lead to delays, unforeseen trade-offs and consequently increase the risk of failure.

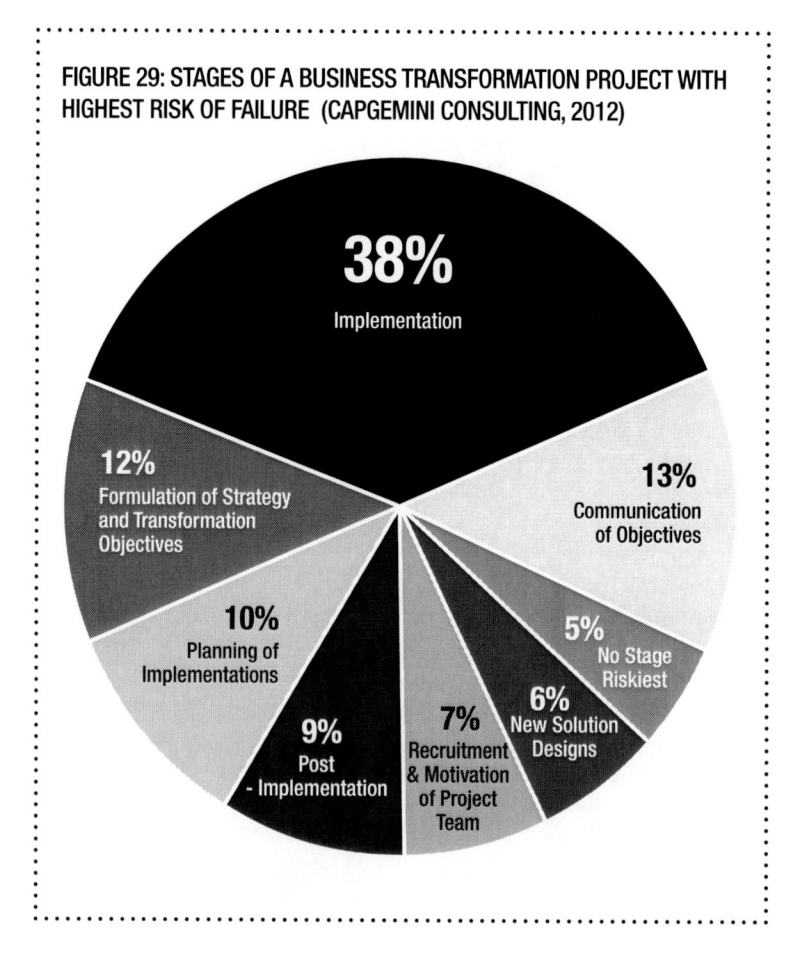

FIGURE 29: STAGES OF A BUSINESS TRANSFORMATION PROJECT WITH HIGHEST RISK OF FAILURE (CAPGEMINI CONSULTING, 2012)

- 38% Implementation
- 13% Communication of Objectives
- 12% Formulation of Strategy and Transformation Objectives
- 10% Planning of Implementations
- 9% Post - Implementation
- 7% Recruitment & Motivation of Project Team
- 6% New Solution Designs
- 5% No Stage Riskiest

3. FAILURE TO WIN OVER EMPLOYEES

Picture the following scenario. A new transformation initiative is launched at an event. The assembled employees nod vigorously in approval whilst the senior management/leadership present the vision. They leave the room, and return to their desks where they discuss the launch - "Another change initiative – I wonder how long this one will last?" Whilst this may sound like an arbitrary example, all too often it represents reality.

In a survey conducted by The Economist, 600 senior management professionals and change experts were interviewed regarding their views on transformation initiatives. Respondents highlighted that the element of change management they found most difficult to deal with was "winning the hearts and minds around required changes" (Economist Intelligence Unit, 2008).

As most professors who deliver lectures on management theory or organisational behaviour will testify, many organisations are inherently averse to change. Organisations are made up of people, and it is the people that inevitably influence whether or not the transformation initiative will be successful, and to what extent.

Figure 30 below also lists "lack of buy-in from local management" and "failure in implementing the agreed strategy and actions" as the second and third most pressing challenges business must deal with.

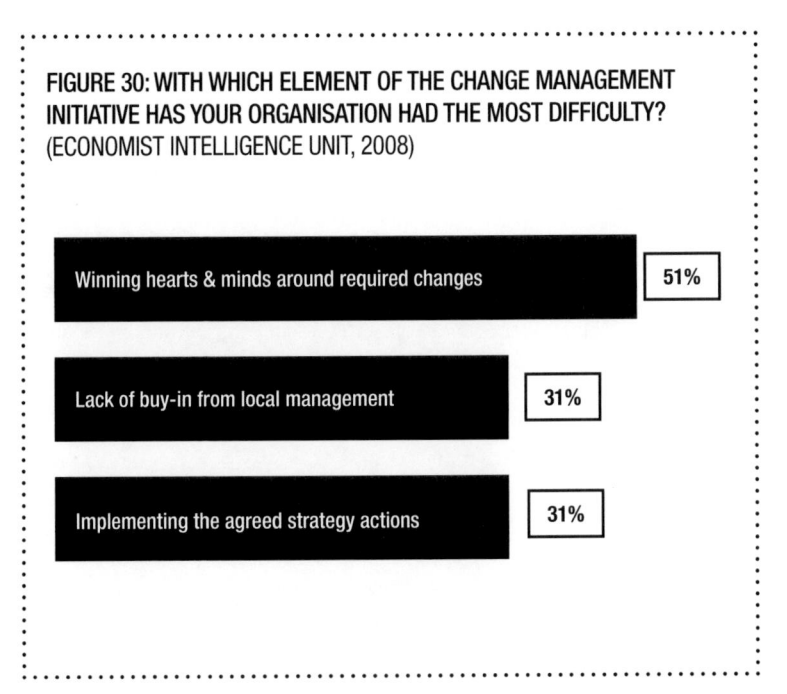

FIGURE 30: WITH WHICH ELEMENT OF THE CHANGE MANAGEMENT INITIATIVE HAS YOUR ORGANISATION HAD THE MOST DIFFICULTY? (ECONOMIST INTELLIGENCE UNIT, 2008)

Element	%
Winning hearts & minds around required changes	51%
Lack of buy-in from local management	31%
Implementing the agreed strategy actions	31%

ENABLERS FOR MAKING TRANSFORMATION A SUCCESS

Having discussed some of the main reasons why transformation initiatives often fail, what can retailers do to avoid becoming another statistic?

1. GETTING THE BASICS RIGHT

When undertaking any transformation initiative, the first question that needs to be answered is, "Why are we doing this?" This may sound obvious, but often posing this simple question can help stakeholders to achieve clarity regarding the drivers of transformation. The creation of quantifiable value should form a key component of the response. Managers, project sponsors and stakeholders involved in the selection and delivery of projects must think in terms of "strategic investments", and senior leadership should be held accountable for delivery. Without this focus, a significant amount of time and money are often wasted on initiatives that fail to achieve their strategic objectives. This ultimately weakens the organisation's competitive position.

Figure 31 overleaf provides a series of prompt questions that might be asked at various stages of the project lifecycle to guide decision making.

2. PUT IN PLACE THE RIGHT LEADERSHIP

Leadership in any transformation initiative is a critical factor in determining success or failure. A study conducted by The Economist noted that the "commitment of senior management" was the single most important factor in determining successful transformation initiatives (Economist Intelligence Unit, 2008). Gaining commitment from the leadership team is a must-have in order to deal with the challenges and issues that arise over the lifecycle of a transformation initiative. Middle management are frequently engaged in the delivery of transformation initiatives, and as a result often do not have the capacity to think strategically and make the big decisions required to steer initiatives towards the delivery of desired outcomes. Senior leaders and management should set the vision, make themselves available to resolve major issues that affect the positive outcome of a project, and instil a culture of "accountability" and "action".

3. CLEAR COMMUNICATION

As mentioned earlier in this chapter, and evidenced by our experience, people are one of the most important components in determining the success of transformation projects. Resistance to change is common and will frequently form when new initiatives are announced. The challenge is how to persuade employees to embrace change in an objective manner, asking, "How can I be a positive force for change, rather than an 'obstacle' in the process?" Leadership is key in instilling an environment where the employee base feel connected to projects and more importantly, the business.

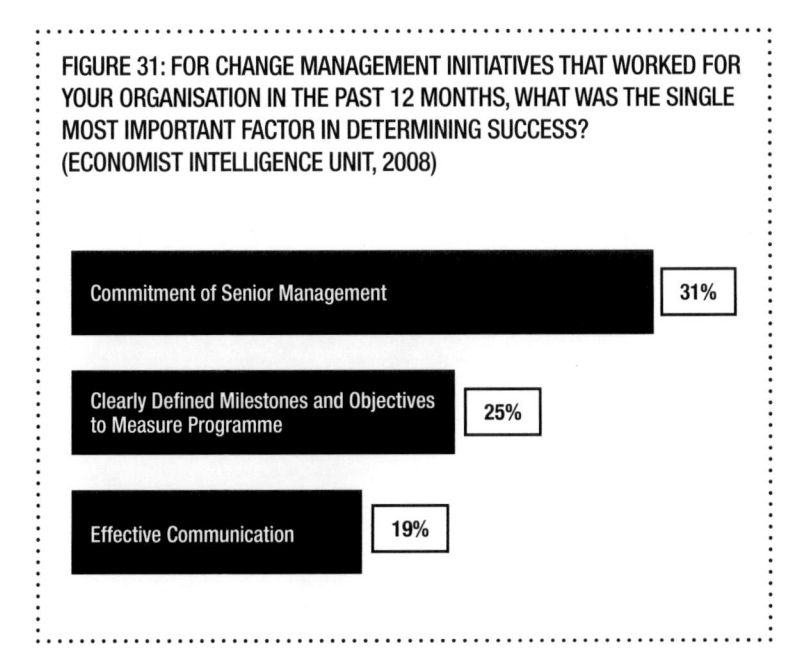

FIGURE 31: FOR CHANGE MANAGEMENT INITIATIVES THAT WORKED FOR YOUR ORGANISATION IN THE PAST 12 MONTHS, WHAT WAS THE SINGLE MOST IMPORTANT FACTOR IN DETERMINING SUCCESS?
(ECONOMIST INTELLIGENCE UNIT, 2008)

Commitment of Senior Management	31%
Clearly Defined Milestones and Objectives to Measure Programme	25%
Effective Communication	19%

KEY QUESTIONS TO ASK DURING THE PROJECT LIFECYCLE

Management need to ask the right questions throughout the project lifecycle in order to ensure that the project achieves the intended outcomes and delivers value to the business. Figure 32 overleaf provides examples of some questions to ask.

EMBEDDING A TRANSFORMATION CULTURE

Transformation is not a one-off exercise but an iterative cycle (see Figure 33). It is important to take the time to work through the steps when formulating the strategic delivery of a project, to communicate frequently in order to keep employees on board and to ensure the right people and mechanisms are in place for the implementation of any initiative.

FIGURE 32: KEY QUESTIONS TO ASK DURING THE PROJECT LIFECYCLE

PROJECT LIFECYCLE PHASE	KEY QUESTIONS
Assess & Plan	<ul><li>Should we invest in the project?</li><li>How do we differentiate between competing projects?</li><li>How do we calculate Return on Investment (ROI) and other business metrics?</li><li>What are important non-ROI-contributing benefits?</li><li>What are the success criteria for this project?</li><li>How can we build the business case and account for the uncertain elements?</li></ul>
Implement	<ul><li>Is the project achieving its intended business objectives?</li><li>How can management help guide the execution to achieve and optimize business objectives?</li><li>Are the key metrics being monitored and reported?</li><li>Does management understand the metrics that are being reported?</li><li>Are the metrics useful?</li><li>Should we continue, modify or even terminate the project?</li></ul>
Post-Implementation Review	<ul><li>Was the project successful?</li><li>Did the project contribute to the company's bottom line?</li><li>Did the project achieve its intended benefits?</li><li>Are we done monitoring and reporting on key project metrics?</li><li>What lessons learned can be garnered from this project?</li></ul>

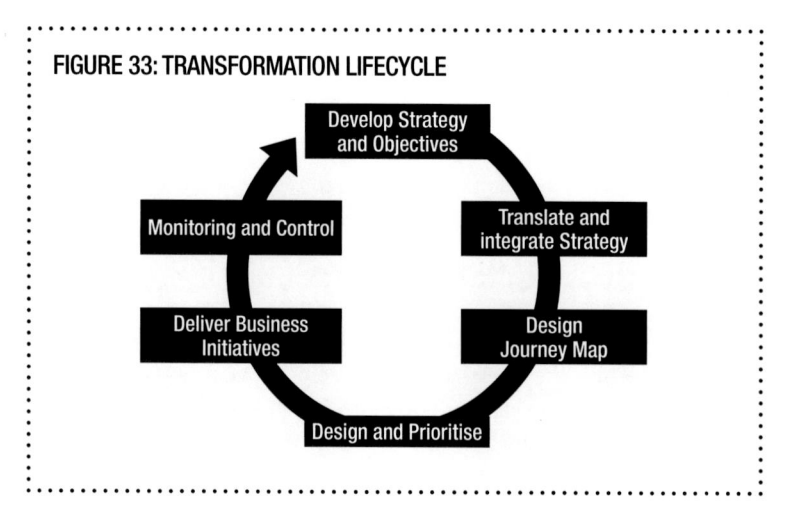

FIGURE 33: TRANSFORMATION LIFECYCLE

- Develop Strategy and Objectives
- Translate and integrate Strategy
- Design Journey Map
- Design and Prioritise
- Deliver Business Initiatives
- Monitoring and Control

CONCLUSION

Transformation and change initiatives are something that all businesses undertake – the only difference being the scale and type of initiatives being run. Taking into account the costs and time spent by employees on transformation initiatives, it is important that organisations make every effort to ensure that the objectives of a particular programme/initiative are realized.

Leadership should cultivate a mind-set whereby all stakeholders involved are determined to get the most out of any transformation/change initiative and are accountable for its success, not just its implementation. More often than not, programmes are measured by whether they were completed within budget, delivered on time and signed off by the appropriate stakeholders. While all these criteria are important, it is imperative that transformation initiatives are measured against the planned return on investment.

Successful transformation initiatives can play a central role in making businesses more competitive, and provide security for the future of the business and its employees. Those that choose to ignore this may be another Kodak in waiting.

KEY TAKEAWAYS:

1. Business transformation initiatives are notorious for not delivering the expected benefits
2. Critical success factors include clear objectives, strong leadership and communication
3. Business transformation programmes must be measured against a quantifiable return on investment

3.2 ORGANISATIONAL EXCELLENCE THROUGH SERVICE MANAGEMENT

AN INTRODUCTION TO SERVICE MANAGEMENT: GREAT SERVICE MAKES OR BREAKS A BUSINESS

THE ONE-MINUTE SERVICE guarantee (your order ready in one minute or your money back) solidified customer views of McDonalds as a reliable brand. Voted "Britain's Favourite Retailer" four years in a row, the quintessentially British John Lewis attributed their success to regular feedback from customer-facing staff to continually improve their service (Wallop, 2010). Virgin Atlantic has developed a reputation for going the extra air mile to provide add-on services such as pre-flight chauffeured limousines and complementary beauty treatments for its upper-class customers (Virgin Atlantic, 2013).

To deliver ongoing excellent service, McDonalds, John Lewis and Virgin Atlantic have all successfully embedded a "service mind-set", a pervasive organisational culture that promotes unwavering dedication to satisfying its clients. The service mind-set is often incomplete, however, without rigorous methodological performance measures and a dedicated service management framework.

EMULATING THE EXTERNAL MARKETPLACE

Service management is defined as the process of proactively managing service provision to a client, inclusive of the tools to measure service quality and overall performance. Importantly, service management transcends industries and empowers an organisation both externally and internally.

Let's explore an example. A client of an advertising agency is assigned an account executive. He or she acts as the central link between the agency and the client to ensure that the former's creative and administrative efforts are addressing the latter's requirements and strategy. Similarly, in the outsourcing industry, an account manager serves as the main point of contact overseeing the relationship between the client and the service provider. In both these examples the account executive and the account manager function as a dedicated service management layer.

For large and complex organisations, who frequently operate separate service production and internal business units, emulating the principles of a service provider-client relationship can help to support the delivery of benefits such as consistent service quality and operational efficiency.

This design principle sits at the heart of the Service Management Framework.

This chapter sets out to describe the building blocks of a service management framework, including how adherence to such a framework adds value to both the top and bottom line, helping to make, rather than break, world-class businesses.

SERVICE MANAGEMENT FRAMEWORK

- An organisation can introduce a service management mind-set by implementing a formalized Service Management Framework;
- A Service Management Framework defines the roles, governance structures, forums, reporting processes and contractual tools that enable service managers to act as the single point of contact for all service-related matters; and
- Service management software tools play an important role in bringing together the building blocks and can help firms with:
  - Effective management of supplier performance;
  - Implementation and rollout of the Service Management Framework; and
  - Improvement of service delivery within an organisation.

Figure 34 below outlines the building blocks of a Service Management Framework.

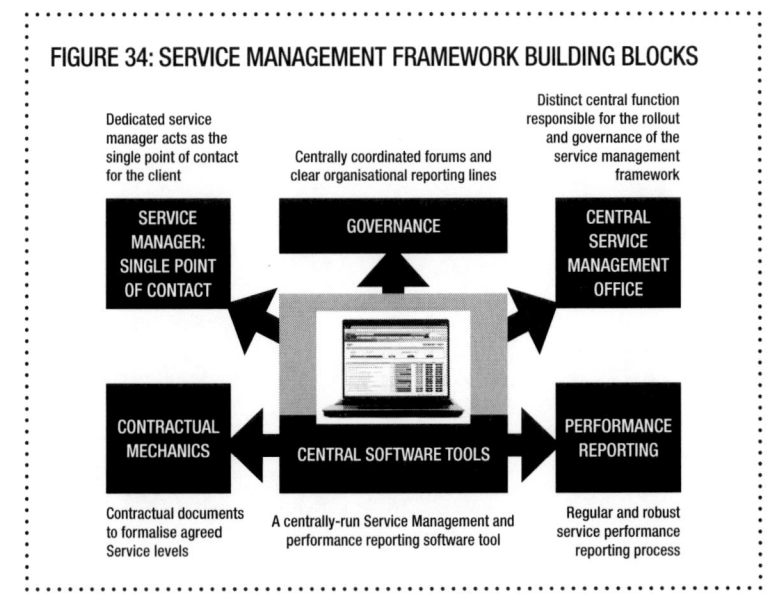

FIGURE 34: SERVICE MANAGEMENT FRAMEWORK BUILDING BLOCKS

SERVICE MANAGER: SINGLE POINT OF CONTACT — Dedicated service manager acts as the single point of contact for the client

GOVERNANCE — Centrally coordinated forums and clear organisational reporting lines

CENTRAL SERVICE MANAGEMENT OFFICE — Distinct central function responsible for the rollout and governance of the service management framework

CONTRACTUAL MECHANICS — Contractual documents to formalise agreed Service levels

CENTRAL SOFTWARE TOOLS — A centrally-run Service Management and performance reporting software tool

PERFORMANCE REPORTING — Regular and robust service performance reporting process

BUILDING BLOCKS AND BENEFITS

Below (see Figure 35) we describe each of the building blocks outlined in Figure 34 in more detail, identifying the benefits of each component.

FIGURE 35: OVERVIEW OF THE KEY BUILDING BLOCKS OF THE SERVICE MANAGEMENT FRAMEWORK

BUILDING BLOCKS	DESCRIPTION	BENEFITS
Service Manager: Single Point of Contact	■ A service management layer within which service managers act as a single point of contact for their internal clients. Their responsibilities include: ■ Establishing strategic partnerships with their client(s) and understanding the strategy ■ Ensuring high levels of service and assisting in offering tailored solutions ■ Challenging client demands and requirements ■ Reviewing service performance metrics to ensure agreed service standards are met ■ Addressing issues of client dissatisfaction	■ Strategic relationships with clients empowers service managers ■ Motivated service managers continually seek ways to improve service ■ Enhanced motivation for service managers further reinforces the service management mind-set ■ Greater responsibility and accountability and linking rewards to performance ■ Faster decision-making process
Contractual Mechanics	■ Contractual mechanics are the contractual tools / documents to enable the organisation to formalize agreed service standard levels to manage robust performance measurement reporting ■ Examples of contractual mechanics include: ■ Master Service Agreement (MSA) – a high-level agreement between the client and service provider ■ Service schedule – the sub-agreements within an MSA which contain more specific service requirements ■ Service Level Agreements (SLAs) – detailed service measures, e.g., time, quality, customer satisfaction, cost, volume, etc. ■ Service catalogue – master document which records a comprehensive list of all services being offered to the client	■ Ability to monitor compliance to Service Level Agreements (SLAs) and measure performance ■ Faster identification and resolution of areas not meeting agreed service levels ■ Embedded culture of regular service levels and contract review to ensure relevancy ■ Consistency of service delivery to help the business focus on attaining its objectives

Governance	■ A well-defined governance structure with clear reporting lines is required ■ Centrally coordinated regular service forums encourage open discussion of service and cost metrics as well as strategic implications	■ Open, clear communication leading to a more proactive relationship ■ Regular forum highlights issues and risks in a timely fashion ■ Visibility of potential conflicts and issues for escalation and prioritization
Performance Reporting	■ Regular and robust performance-reporting processes ■ Service metrics are reported and highlighted in dashboards to management ■ A central dashboard will roll up the Red, Amber, Green (RAG) status and key performance metrics from each area to the Executive Committee or other senior management tiers as appropriate	■ Consistency in reporting methodology across the organisation ■ Instil mind-set and routine of regularly measuring and monitoring service levels
Central Service Management Office (CSMO)	■ A distinct Central Service Management Office (CSMO) function, inclusive of a service management office lead, is responsible for the overall governance of the service management framework within an organisation ■ Responsibilities of the CSMO include: 　■ Supporting service management forums 　■ Providing oversight on alignment of the service management framework 　■ Providing guidance and direction 　■ Providing a repository for maintaining overarching contractual mechanics documentation ■ Responsibilities of the CSMO lead include: 　■ Delivering the rollout of the service management framework across an organisation 　■ Providing guidance and direction to service managers	■ Central coordination and alignment of the service management framework ■ Ensures consistency in approach ■ Greater efficiency by leveraging economies of scale

Central Software Tools	<ul><li>A centrally run integrated reporting and performance software tool can help to monitor and track service performance</li><li>Automated dashboards provide greater visibility and consolidation of service reporting</li><li>A document vault acts as central depository house and provides document management system</li><li>Automatic alert and email notification when service levels agreements are not met</li></ul>	<ul><li>Real-time and up-to-date comprehensive management information</li><li>Ease of use and drill-down functionality</li><li>Facilitates comparison of service level RAG status between locations or business areas</li></ul>

THE KEYS TO ORGANISATIONAL EXCELLENCE

CONTINUOUS IMPROVEMENT AND INNOVATION

Implementing a service management framework to facilitate the relationship between internal clients and service provision units can help to deliver an overall service mind-set or culture, which can ultimately deliver operational efficiency and productivity. Consequently, the organisation as a whole can experience higher levels of client satisfaction (both internally and externally) whilst improving profitability and margin, as a result of greater efficiencies. Primarily, these pillars of organisational success are achieved by a strong and proactive service management ethos which promotes ongoing continuous improvement and innovation.

CONTINUOUS IMPROVEMENT

Continuous improvement is a result of a virtuous cycle that encourages ownership and proactivity by Service Managers themselves. Rather than having a process imposed upon them from a central department, the service management mind-set encourages Service Managers to act as the client's strategic partners. Sitting in the client's key meetings, Service Managers are at the heart of their client's plans and strategies to improve service performance. This recognised pivotal role motivates Service Managers to take ownership and commit to raising service levels.

Continually seeking to improve service performance often involves small step changes rather than large-scale radical transformation. These are often faster, more straightforward to implement and require less capital investment. These small step changes might include more robust monitoring of quantitative metrics, as well as enhanced communication and feedback to identify service improvement areas. Greater transparency and accountability allow Service Managers to be individually recognised and rewarded, thus furthering the support of the service management mind-set, and fostering another cycle of continuous improvement.

INNOVATION

At the same time, innovation has a role to play as a key differentiator. Service management plays a critical role in introducing and maintaining innovation throughout the organisation. Through closer strategic relationships with clients, Service Managers are best placed to take advantage of "innovation triggers" which occur through their direct interaction with the end customer, providing feedback and suggestions to the "front office" service management. Other innovation triggers include the front office staff's observation of client trends and behaviour, as well as his or her own awareness of new technology and competitor activities. These innovation triggers filter down through the organisation to the internal business units and their Service Managers who, in turn, relay these to the service production functions.

Subsequently, innovative ideas and projects are stimulated, adding value from both a product development and process improvement perspective.

Innovation in products is experienced by the end customers through innovative product ideas, or ways to expand market share or enter new markets, including enhanced service capabilities.

Innovation in process takes place within an organisation's operations, and is often technology-driven or involves deploying a fresh business process to improve cost-efficiency. In both these instances, service management is the fuel that keeps an organisation's innovation engine running.

CONCLUSION

To stay ahead of the game, companies can no longer afford to turn a blind eye to service management – it has become commonplace, whether the result of a deliberate effort or not, across all industries. Ultimately, a true appreciation of service management and how to cultivate this mind-set towards both external and internal clients will be the key to sustaining organisational excellence and delivering cost-efficiencies, innovation and exemplary service.

FIGURE 36: ORGANISATIONAL EXCELLENCE THROUGH SERVICE MANAGEMENT

Service Management is most effective when implemented through a formalized Service Management Framework, which defines the roles, governance structure, forums, reporting processes and contractual tools, enabling Service Managers to act as the single point of contact to their clients.

BENEFIT ▼

| Emulating a common practice in the external marketplace and implementing service management within an organisation can help achieve operational efficiency and improve operating margins. | Service management leads to greater compliance to agreed service levels and regulations, consistency in delivering service and faster identification of areas not meeting agreed service standards. | Cultivating a service management mind-set in an organisation drives a culture of ongoing continuous improvement and innovation – the two key pillars of organisational excellence. |

KEY TAKEAWAYS:

1. In order to support the adoption of a "service" mind-set, organisations should consider adopting a Service Management Framework
2. Software tools can play a role in delivering the benefits of each of the key building blocks of the Service Management Framework
3. Service management is just as important for managing internal functions as it is for external clients and customers

3.3 REMOVING THE "T" FROM YOUR TOM

HOW CAN A BUSINESS make sure that a Target Operating Model (TOM) design will become a reality and not collect dust while the business strategy moves in another direction?

This focuses on how to design a TOM that meets business needs and actually gets implemented – and hence is no longer a Target. We provide experience-based insight on each of the steps that need to be taken to achieve a successful TOM design.

WHAT IS A TOM?
A TOM is a design for the way a business (or part of it) should operate to best execute its strategy and objectives. It comprises the required functions and capabilities ("the what"), as well as who, where and how these are delivered. Underpinning the TOM is the associated organisational design.

WHY IS THIS RELEVANT RIGHT NOW?
Many organisations are addressing their operating model for the following compelling reasons:

1. ECONOMIC SITUATION
In these times of relative austerity, organisations are cutting costs and seeking out efficiencies, often via an operating model overhaul.

2. EVER-MORE DYNAMIC ENVIRONMENT
Today's business environment is increasingly dynamic and therefore traditional ways of operating are frequently ill-prepared to adapt to rapidly changing external factors.

3. AGILITY AND EXPANSION
Many established markets are saturated, so organisations need to be able to identify and exploit new opportunities in new industries and markets – the ability to roll out quickly is imperative.

FIGURE 37: ELIX-IRR'S TOM METHODOLOGY

This chapter uses our tried and tested TOM design methodology as a structure through which to provide practical insight into making TOM design a success.

1	2	3	4	5	6	7	8
Business & Operational Strategy Alignment	Component Architecture Design	Service Management Framework	Location Strategy	Organisation Design & Governance	Business Benefits & Investment Case	Sourcing Strategy	Implementation Roadmap

The following eight design steps (Figure 38) are based on Elix-IRR's experience and provide a proven methodology for successfully designing operating models:

FIGURE 38: TOM DESIGN STEPS

STEP	KEY MESSAGES
1. Business & Operational Alignment ■ Clearly articulate the business strategy – get all stakeholders to confirm agreement before commencing any design ■ Business strategy will evolve over time – check periodically to remain aligned ■ Senior advocacy is required – someone with the right level of seniority and respect amongst the affected stakeholders is needed to generate momentum and buy-in ■ TOM designs will have an impact on many stakeholders, but the design team must be compact and focused to ensure traction - they must be mandated for the wider group	■ Ensure clarity on business strategy and its implications for the TOM ■ Provide proactive leadership from a senior champion acting as an advocate
2. Component Architecture Design ■ Collaborative, face-to-face process to agree the design principles and obtain real buy-in ■ The design principles must be clearly aligned to the business strategy, and unambiguous with no room for interpretation – they will be the "reference point" for all future design decisions ■ Use an iterative design process – the priorities will change – but these iterations must be within a set framework of "immovable principles" ■ The scope and content of each component of the architecture needs to be defined and documented	■ Define clear TOM design principles ■ Define scope and content of each component ■ Robust documentation is a must

3. Service Management Framework
- A "service mind-set" must be instilled – backed by internal and external service levels
- Be clear on each component's internal and external customers, as well as those components it is itself a customer of
- Understand the importance of the service manager role in managing supply and demand – requiring a unique set of skills
- Changes may be needed to cost centres and finance processes to enable recharging
- Ensure service transparency through appropriate reporting tools

- Define service manager roles and responsibilities
- Define appropriate SLAs to manage supply and demand

4. Location Strategy
- Rigorous analysis of delivery model options is needed to select the most appropriate one
- For multi-country TOMs, be sensitive to political issues – regional hubs will impact on personal spheres of influence and growth opportunities for in-country leaders
- If looking to consolidate or centralize, the default position must be just that – any variation justified and managed through a design authority
- Understand the real reasons that require a service to be delivered locally – not just the emotional or subjective reasons given by those resisting change

- Consider all factors – internal and external – when assessing locations
- Take the emotion out of location decisions

5. Organisation Design and Governance
- Establish a Design Authority to own design principles and key design decisions
- Understand who the key players are – get them on board and the others will follow
- Establish a clear set of Organisational Design Principles to apply both centrally and in-country (if appropriate)
- Document responsibilities and accountabilities of senior roles
- Empower those in key roles – get division owners to design their desired organisation structures and then integrate into one agreed organisation design
- Appropriate governance, not bureaucracy

- Have the right level of visible sponsorship
- Governance model for design should evolve into "BAU" structure

6. Business Benefits & Investment Case
- Business case must be iterative – building out more detail as the design progresses
- Many benefits will be intangible, so go-ahead for design should be given on buy-in to the concept. Subsequent, costly implementation phases require a "hard" business case
- Investment costs must be clearly articulated – these are difficult to predict at the outset and are often overlooked
- Key dependencies, risks and issues need to be identified and mitigations outlined
- 3rd parties (suppliers) can be used to assist with funding issues

- Articulate investment costs, key dependencies, risks and issues
- Identify revenue opportunities to help bolster business case

7. Sourcing Strategy - Only investigate the "who" when the "what" and the "how" have been agreed - Understand where 3rd parties could help with capability and/or capacity deficits - Understand impacts of outsourcing entire functions (including management) – the marginal labour arbitrage benefit might be outweighed by the loss of control and business intelligence - Develop a consistent framework for sourcing opportunities - Establish a strong vendor management function, fully integrated into a business-wide service management model	- Understand "what good looks like" before engaging 3rd parties - Avoid scope "creep" but use additional scope as incentive
8. Implementation Roadmap - Be clear on "what good looks like" before implementation starts - Incorporate quick wins to demonstrate early success and build momentum - Achieve critical mass of stakeholder buy-in required to start - Appropriately balance risk, control, cost and reward throughout the roadmap - Implementation plans should be split according to short/medium/long phases with appropriate level of detail for each - Develop TOM blueprints and implementation handbooks to standardize country rollouts	- Prioritize the most valuable areas – don't try to do it all at once - Define transitional operating models to break up the journey

CONCLUSION

Making a TOM design "stick" and become a reality is difficult, but with the right approach and awareness of the common pitfalls, it can be done. Elix-IRR believes that by adhering to the following three tenets, organisations can greatly increase their chances of creating a valuable and practicable TOM design.

FIGURE 39: 3 CORE TENETS OF TOM DESIGN

Invest time up-front – agree the principles	The key stakeholders (and future owners of the model) must have participated in the development and signed off the design principles
Demonstrate success early on	Transforming the way a business operates can take time, so build momentum and belief by delivering tangible success in the early stages
Advocacy, not just sponsorship	A "perfect" design will fail if it does not have the support of key decision makers. Senior sponsorship is not enough – proactive advocacy is required

KEY TAKEAWAYS:

1. A Target Operating Model (TOM) is a design for the way a business (or part of it) should operate to best execute its strategy and objectives
2. Elix-IRR has developed an eight-step methodology for TOM design
3. Investing time in establishing principles, demonstrating success early on and creating advocates are common elements of successful TOM implementations

4.
OUTSOURCING IN RETAIL

CHAPTER OVERVIEW

In this chapter, we discuss the opportunities and challenges relevant to outsourcing in retail. Whilst outsourcing can be a divisive topic for retail executives, the value of a well-managed outsourcing contract should not be underestimated. In this chapter, we examine the opportunity in the wake of the recent recession and discuss strategies to manage the delivery of potential benefits. We also cover the rise of "nearshoring" as an alternative to traditional outsourcing models, before discussing why the traditional Request for Proposal (RFP) approach to selecting vendor partners may not be as optimal as some suggest, and that there are alternatives, such as Elix-IRR's Collaborative Solutioning methodology.

4.1 OUTSOURCING: DELIVERING THE EXPECTED BENEFITS

There has been much debate in the media about whether outsourcing truly delivers on the expected benefits, with some prominent publications suggesting that outsourcing is sometimes more hassle than it is worth. The reality is that some deals will be set up and managed well, while others may be a disaster for the client, vendor or both.

Key to success is aligning the goals of both client and vendor, incentivizing the vendor to do what the client requires, and setting up the deal to ensure this happens. In this chapter, we focus on how to ensure success in an outsourcing project by following five simple steps.

4.2 THE RISE OF "NEARSHORING"

As the economic pressures of the recent recession are still being felt in most of the developed world, offshoring and outsourcing remain key levers for most major corporates in trying to reduce their cost base.

However, with local political pressure intensifying against sending jobs offshore, and many of the typical offshore destinations continuing to experience double-digit rates of inflation, are there any alternatives closer to home that cost-conscious executives can explore?

4.3 RETAIL IT SOURCING TODAY

How do retailers source technology today, and what impact might industry and technology trends have on their IT sourcing approach?

Large transformational outsourcing deals are not as prevalent within retail as in other sectors such as Financial Services and the Public Sector. This section describes the current Retail IT sourcing environment and how this is evolving due to factors such as changing consumer habits and the availability of new technologies. This chapter highlights how effective IT sourcing can deliver benefits to retailers, all of which can help to deliver an improved bottom line, and how the need for innovation in the age of internet shopping is driving change in the IT sourcing landscape for retail.

4.4 TO RFP OR NOT TO RFP? USING COLLABORATIVE SOURCING AS A VIABLE ALTERNATIVE

When embarking upon an outsourcing journey, most advisors in the market today will suggest putting the bid out to tender amongst suppliers. Requests for Proposal (RFPs) can be an efficient way of comparing vendors in terms of commercials and agreement to contractual terms.

But they are also an efficient way of making sourcing advisors healthy margins, delaying the business case by up to a year, and of disconnecting the solution from the original strategic intent. Whilst the RFP process certainly has a time and a place, it should not be the default journey companies embark upon. Indeed, often it is simply the wrong commercial decision.

4.1 OUTSOURCING: DELIVERING THE EXPECTED BENEFITS

OUTSOURCING IS A BIG INDUSTRY in its own right – in 2011 in the UK, it had become almost as big as the financial services sector, generating over £200 billion a year and employing 10% of the British workforce (Spence, 2011). There has been much debate in the media about whether outsourcing truly delivers on the expected benefits, with some prominent publications suggesting that outsourcing is sometimes more hassle than it is worth (The Economist, 2011).

The reality is that some deals will be set up and managed well, while others may be a disaster for the client, vendor or both. Key to success is aligning the goals of both client and vendor, incentivizing the vendor to do what the client requires and setting up the deal to ensure this happens. In this section, we focus on how to ensure success in an outsourcing project by following five simple steps:

FIGURE 40: THE FIVE STEPS TO ENSURING OUTSOURCING SUCCESS

STEP	DESCRIPTION
1. Align sourcing requirements to strategy	Ensuring that the deal is aligned to the needs of an organisation, whether it is a large multinational enterprise or a small government department
2. Design the "Target Operating Model" (TOM)	The TOM sets out how the organisation should be designed, so as to effectively manage the vendor and extract the most value from the deal. It sets out the functions and activities that should be retained by the client and the governance frameworks for how the vendor will be managed
3. Agree the sourcing strategy	The sourcing strategy should explain exactly what should be outsourced, why and how. Should one vendor deliver everything and sub-contract other companies as required, or should the client manage multiple vendor relationships simultaneously? Should there be open competition (generally a requirement for public sector organisations), or should the client start negotiations with one or more carefully selected vendors?
4. Ensure the deal is set up for success	It is relatively easy to ensure that the services to be delivered are accurately described within the contract, and to set up the right governance to ensure that service quality is maintained. However, in reality it is harder to ensure that the vendor is incentivized to meet or exceed quality and cost expectations

5. Be ready for change, and plan for the end	All outsourcing deals will have an "expiry date", but some deals go sour before the end. A deal that does not have flexibility and scalability to meet changes in business requirements, technology and the market is unlikely to be fit for purpose by the end of the deal

ALL OUTSOURCING DEALS ARE DIFFERENT

There is no single way to approach an outsourcing deal, as each one is different. One organisation might only seek to outsource its IT support function, whilst another might want to outsource almost everything, just like the UK's National Savings and Investments did in 1999 as it transferred all IT, most business processes and 98% of its staff to Siemens. If an outsourcing project involves many different functions, multiple countries and sites, and several vendors, then deal complexity increases. It is these types of larger and more complex deals that we present an approach for in this section, although the principles we discuss can be adopted for most deals.

WHO IS GOING TO RUN THE PROCESS?

One word of caution, though – while reading about "making an outsourcing deal work" will certainly help, do not forget that you will be negotiating with experienced "deal teams" from vendors who are continually shaping and negotiating deals favourable to the vendor.

In the same way that you cannot expect an infrequent flyer to land a 747 safely, you should not expect an internal sourcing team to land the best deal on their own. If the organisation wants to quickly secure the best outcome with the least risk, then they should strongly consider engaging professional advisors to help them navigate through the outsourcing journey and land the right deal.

1. ALIGNING SOURCING REQUIREMENTS TO STRATEGY
WHY OUTSOURCE ANYWAY?

Although most people think that the main reason organisations outsource is to reduce costs – for example, through labour arbitrage and the offshoring of domestic labour to another country where labour is cheaper – this is not the only or main reason to outsource.

Being clear on the strategic intent of the deal is key to success. All organisations want to improve the "bottom line" and generate shareholder returns, but cutting costs is just part of the profit equation.

For companies new to an emerging market, faster market entry and outpacing their competitors are important goals. For example, if a company wants to quickly build their presence in an emerging economy such as Angola, it may outsource provision of facilities to a local company, and engage a local vendor to rapidly supply infrastructure such as data centres and networks.

Some organisations may lack the capital to refresh technology, or need to overcome a shortage of particular skills. For example, a high-street company whose focus for years has been on building and maintaining complex legacy mainframe systems may want to expand further into the internet marketplace. Rather than hire or train individual developers with the requisite web 2.0 and agile skills, it may consider outsourcing the job to a vendor able to build and run a transactional website, perhaps on a resilient platform shared by other internet companies.

STRATEGIC SOURCING

However, a few people in some organisations may be thinking more strategically and looking to generate shareholder value through creating and commercializing an asset. For example, a bank may seek to generate value through setting up a financial services company whereby operations can be shared by a number of organisations. The shared services company would be set up to manage non-competitive operations of the bank such as the clearing and settlement of payments, and offer that function as a service to other organisations. This would not only improve economies of scale, but given the right commercial structure, it could create an asset with realizable value.

The nature and scope of an outsourcing deal, and whether it is tactical or strategic, is dependent on who raises the opportunity within an organisation and how widely engaged the management team is. For example, a human resources manager may only have the remit to outsource a payroll function, whereas a company board may consider more strategic options of outsourcing multiple business processes and IT.

> **TIP:** The value that can be unlocked by an outsourcing deal is closely related to how strategic and game-changing the opportunity is. But strategic deals are by their nature more complex than simple single-function deals, and are harder to design and manage. This is where designing a TOM for an organisation becomes essential.

2. DESIGNING THE TARGET OPERATING MODEL (TOM)
WHAT IS A TOM FOR?
Put simply, the TOM should show how the capability and functions of a business should be structured to help achieve the business strategy. A good TOM should illustrate how parts of a business are configured, so as to help make and communicate decisions such as:
- Which capabilities and functions should the business have, and what is currently missing? For example, within IT operations, comparison against good practice models (e.g., ITIL) may expose missing functions such as a "help desk" or the ability to properly manage change.
- How should the different parts of the business be designed in terms of number of people, budget and location?
- How are services delivered to customers of the business, and how does the organisation manage vendors that help us provide those services?

BUILD VS. BUY
Once the capabilities and functions have been defined, the sourcing strategy can then outline whether it would be better to build capability within an organisation, or whether a decision to source from the market (i.e., outsourcing) would be better for the business. This can be done on a tactical basis for a specific capability (e.g., IT outsourcing for networks provision or for specific BPO functions such as a call centre), or on a more strategic basis by looking to outsource more capabilities and functions at the same time. Ultimately a "build versus buy" decision is made and the organisation should be clear on what to outsource.

OFF-THE-SHELF VS. CUSTOM-BUILT
Where outsourcing involves well-defined functions such as a data centre or contact centre, the market is often correspondingly well defined and therefore highly competitive: service descriptions and pricing schedules have been refined over many years, benchmarking has helped to drive the pricing down and there will be plenty of vendors knocking on the door offering good deals. A simple transactional deal to buy a range of commodity services might be all that is required.

However, at the opposite end of the spectrum, unusual combinations of functions will mean there are fewer vendors capable of delivering the total requirement. This in turn will mean less competition and a weaker market response, resulting in higher-risk premiums and less competitive pricing that is harder to benchmark. In these situations, it is sensible to encourage and allow the market to respond freely to requirements, rather than force a particular business model or relationship. It is in these complex deals where consortiums amongst bidders, partnering and joint venture possibilities are more likely to be explored.

> **TIP:** A TOM must also describe how the outsourcing vendor will be managed. It should identify the functions and roles that will be required to manage the ongoing vendor relationship once the deal is signed.

OUTSOURCING IN EMERGING MARKETS OFTEN REQUIRES A PARTNERSHIP APPROACH

Africa, for example, has a less developed outsourcing market than Europe and the US, and to encourage international vendors to explore a deal and potentially enter the market for the first time, an organisation may be willing to establish a joint venture with an outsourcer. That way, transformation and improvement across a range of functions can be delivered at a lower investment than if the organisation were to improve its operations on its own. Partnering with a vendor highly experienced in delivering a particular function such as payroll is a good way to drive improvement quickly and cost-effectively.

AFTER THE DEAL IS SIGNED…

In several organisations, it is common to have a project team set up to negotiate the deal and put a little thought into how the deal will be managed on an ongoing basis. Ideally, an organisation should establish a strong vendor management team with the right tools (for example, to manage contracts and service level agreements (SLAs)). If vendor management is weak, then over time the deal is likely to diverge from its original business case.

For example, in a large retail banking deal signed over 10 years ago, an organisation outsourced all of its IT as part of outsourcing many of its key business processes. There was little consideration as to how it would continue to be "an intelligent client" once all of its IT people were transferred to the outsourcer. Commercial experts had assumed that they could manage the contract, but over time there were many variations to the contract and a real need for IT expertise to ensure solutions proposed by the vendor were fit for purpose and represented value for money. Eventually, an "IS assurance" function was created to help manage these aspects, and to ensure that the vendor delivered on key IT commitments as part of the original deal.

FIGURE 41: EXAMPLE TOM FOR FACILITIES MANAGEMENT, GROUPING THE LOCATION OF FUNCTIONS

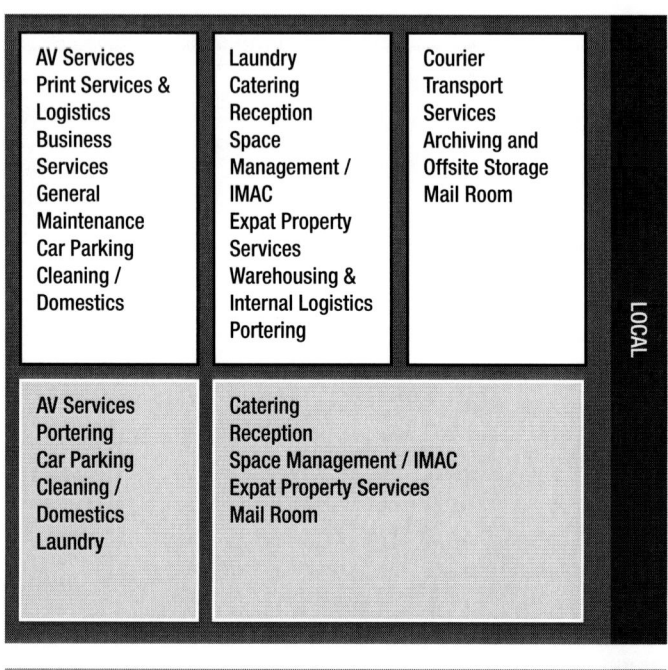

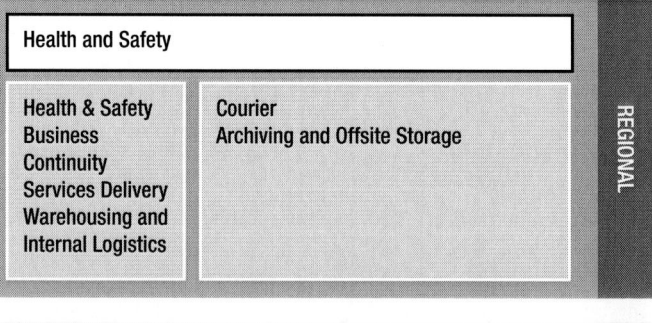

LOCAL

AV Services
Print Services & Logistics
Business Services
General Maintenance
Car Parking
Cleaning / Domestics

Laundry
Catering
Reception
Space Management / IMAC
Expat Property Services
Warehousing & Internal Logistics
Portering

Courier
Transport Services
Archiving and Offsite Storage
Mail Room

AV Services
Portering
Car Parking
Cleaning / Domestics
Laundry

Catering
Reception
Space Management / IMAC
Expat Property Services
Mail Room

REGIONAL

Health and Safety

Health & Safety
Business Continuity
Services Delivery
Warehousing and Internal Logistics

Courier
Archiving and Offsite Storage

CENTRAL

Building Service

Print and Logistics
General Maintenance

FM Specialized & Sourcing

Centralized Governance for All Functions

3. AGREE THE SOURCING STRATEGY
PRIVATE VS. PUBLIC SECTOR
The private sector has a key advantage over the public sector in that it can be much more flexible in how it engages the market. Within the public sector, there are defined rules and processes to follow, with the good intention of getting the best deal for the taxpayer – although when the length and cost of the procurement process is factored in, the taxpayer may not agree. For example, within Europe there is the Official Journal of the European Union (OJEU) where all tenders from the public sector above a particular financial threshold must be published, and a particular procurement process followed (e.g., open, restricted or negotiated).

Private sector organisations can instead define their own shortlist of vendors away from public scrutiny, and engage in negotiations with one or more vendors at a far quicker pace. This has the advantage of protecting corporate strategies and accelerating benefits delivery as the vendor selection process is typically much quicker (e.g., for an outsourcing deal covering one or two functions, vendor selection could take three to six months in the private sector, but 18 months or more in the public sector, delaying benefits by more than 12 months).

MARKET ENGAGEMENT MODEL
When dealing with private sector outsourcing, there is great flexibility as to how to engage the market. Factors that will influence the chosen approach include:
- Internal procurement policies and guidelines;
- The existence of a "burning platform", such as an existing contract that is about to expire;
- Availability of the services from the market – commodity services such as IT support are readily available, and competition can be used to drive down price;
- How well defined the requirements are, and how well the client understands what can be outsourced – early engagement with the market through a "Request for Information" (RFI) process can be beneficial here; and
- Commercial sensitivities – for example, knowledge of the need for services to support new market expansion is probably best kept away from competitors, so early dialogue and negotiation with a select few vendors may be the best approach.

Despite the UK government wanting its own procurement teams to engage more with suppliers, many vendors find out about an opportunity through a public notice – and it is up to them to respond (Flinders, Francis Maude is unashamedly obsessed with procurement but what's in it for suppliers?, 2011). However, in the private sector the client can ensure specific vendors are alerted to an opportunity – but which vendors should be approached?

This is where external expertise from sourcing advisors can be beneficial. With experience of multiple vendors and deals, and with a blend of vendor, buyer and consulting skills, they can be valuable matchmakers. Beyond just ensuring a good fit between client and vendor, advisors can help shape and position a deal for the benefit of both parties.

START AS YOU MEAN TO GO ON

Getting the best deal is important, but if the cultural and relationship fit between client and vendor is not strong, the marriage may end in divorce as there will likely be many more negotiations long after the deal is struck.

In an ideal situation, the client will know exactly what it is outsourcing – the scope will be clear, asset registers will be accurate and service quality expectations will be reasonable and based on actual historical management reports. However, this ideal situation is rare, especially in organisations new to outsourcing. For example, one European bank that outsourced its facilities management services for the first time was vague about exactly what was outsourced and had no accurate list of branches to be serviced, no asset register and no established history of service level performance.

The implication of the client being vague and flexible on requirements and scope is that vendors pitching for their business will factor in lots of uncertainty and risk into the deal – and risk comes with a cost. So, if a client wants to reduce the risk premium it pays and have a stronger contract, it should invest time and effort up-front to drive out ambiguity and clearly define and document the scope of what will be outsourced and the service quality it expects. These aspects can always be negotiated, but at least there will be a common and well-understood starting point for negotiations.

OUTSOURCING "PROBLEM AREAS"

There is a long-running debate among outsourcing professionals about the pros and cons of outsourcing a problem area ("your mess for less" versus sorting out the mess before outsourcing). Outsourcing a mess can be done relatively quickly, and is preferred by many outsourcing vendors. They will proclaim to have "done that kind of transformation before" and have the skills necessary to map out the current processes, design a better way of working and deliver the improvements required. However, unless they have invested hugely in due diligence they will not know the exact situation they are getting themselves into, and are likely to price in a significant risk premium.

Sorting out the mess first takes a lot longer to secure benefits as it delays the outsourcing deal itself. It also reduces the upside for vendors, but is preferred by consultancies, many of which have built large businesses from helping clients to map processes and document everything ahead of any deal. The problem is that it can take so long that significant costs can be incurred – both from actual consultancy fees and from the opportunity cost of delayed outsourcing benefits.

Neither of these extremes is usually best for the client – there is a balance to be struck that will be different for each client situation.

4. ENSURE THE DEAL IS SET UP FOR SUCCESS

The deal should be set up so that vendors are motivated to deliver the desired client outcomes, which may include cost reduction, service quality improvement, customer satisfaction targets or even the replacement or development of infrastructure. In this section, we discuss various incentivization techniques, the aim of which is to encourage desired vendor behaviours, relationships and outcomes.

ENSURING SERVICE QUALITY

Many readers will be familiar with the concepts of Service Level Agreements (SLAs), Key Performance Indicators (KPIs), and other similar measures of service quality. The basic premise is that measures of service quality and targets important to the client are defined and agreed as part of the deal, so that if the vendor does not achieve the desired service levels, then through a performance credits regime, vendor costs are reduced.

Do not leave it until after the deal is in place – and if possible avoid a waiver of performance credits in the early months of a deal. This is often sought by vendors where there is no track record of service quality, and is one way for them to reduce financial risk. For example, one IT vendor the authors negotiated with boldly asked for a waiver of SLAs for the first 12 months of a 3-year deal.

> **TIP:** A good service management framework is important for "business as usual" operations, as it helps the vendor focus on delivering what is important to the client. If a deal involves standard operational activities such as processing payments, keeping a service available or cleaning facilities, then an SLA regime should be agreed before signing the deal.

However, performance credits are a "stick" rather than a "carrot" approach, in that vendors will strive to avoid a financial penalty for poor performance. Often there is no positive incentive to over-perform or innovate, and the cost of allocating resources to deliver beyond agreed service targets would eat into vendor profit margins. It can also lead to the wrong behaviours if vendors focus resources to deliver against the few measures where there are penalties, to the detriment of delivering other aspects of a deal.

ALTERNATIVE INCENTIVIZATION APPROACHES

So what other incentivization approaches are available, and do they really work? Some of the more common techniques include:

- Payment at risk or reward – the key word here is "reward" for the vendor, as opposed to just the "risk" they get with performance credits. For example, in an IT development deal, if the vendor were to achieve a development and testing milestone early, or exceed the agreed scope and quality, then they could receive additional bonus payments;
- Gain/pain share – may allow a vendor to keep a share of financial benefits they have helped the client to achieve. For example, a UK bank that had outsourced its call-centre operations as part of a wider BPO deal encouraged the sale of its products by paying the vendor a fee for each product sold by call-centre agents; and
- Contingency funds – where additional contingency funds are allocated to a project during budget planning to help manage both identified risks and unforeseen events. Vendors are incentivized to more effectively manage risk, as the unspent proportion of the contingency fund may be shared between the client and vendor as a form of reward.

RISK OR REWARD DEALS

"Risk or reward" deals are fairly easy to comprehend and agree up-front, but far more difficult to manage in practice. Sometimes clients do not fully think through the implications of some of the incentive mechanisms and how they may translate into a lack of desired outcomes.

For example, during one large IT outsourcing deal for the development of a high-volume payments system, "milestone payments" meant that if development and testing milestones were delayed, then payment would also be delayed. There was a detailed "acceptance criteria" list for key milestones, but the vendor was not achieving all criteria for acceptance and was demanding payment. Contractually, the client had the right to withhold all payment until delivery was formally accepted. In reality, what happened was the vendor applied pressure along the lines of "if we are not paid, then we will lose some of our most talented contractors, and that will jeopardize delivery even further".

The client eventually succumbed and paid over 80% of the milestone payment, losing significant negotiation leverage in the process. The subsequent milestones were also delivered late, and more effort was spent on negotiating part payments – instead of focusing on the root causes of delay, which included poor programme management, changes of scope and lack of firm requirements. The main outcome of quality solutions being delivered on time was not achieved.

GAIN AND PAIN SHARE DEALS

"Gain and pain share" can be implemented in many different ways. For example, within a multi-billion-dollar defence contract, there were gain share provisions – the theory being that if the vendor identified potential cost savings, then they could take a share as a reward. The reality was that despite three proposals from the vendor for initiatives to reduce cost, the two parties never reached agreement on a cost-savings proposal. The vendor was frustrated that the effort they spent was wasted as nothing was accepted, and the client believed that the quality of the proposals was insufficient to warrant implementation. A root cause of the disagreement was the lack of an agreed cost baseline against which any savings could be measured.

In summary, the key to getting a vendor to behave and deliver as desired is to have the right commercial model and financial incentives in place, and a combination of different incentivization techniques to cover the full scope of different outsourced functions and services is likely to be the optimal solution.

5. BE READY FOR CHANGE, AND PLAN FOR THE END
MANAGING CHANGE

Given that most outsourcing deals run for terms of between three and ten years, the only thing that can be guaranteed between the time of signing a deal and its natural end is that there will be many changes in between. Therefore, it is critical that change is planned for and managed effectively – and that includes the transition that occurs at the end of a contract, whether it ends prematurely or as planned.

For example, a change in regulations or market demand for a product, altering the scope of an IT development or the client moving office will all result in a change requirement. The vendor is usually asked to assess the impact of the changes, and submit a pricing proposal. Whereas the client sees many changes as an additional and often unplanned cost that must be controlled, the vendor usually sees change as a great opportunity to generate additional revenue.

PREPARING FOR LARGE-IMPACT CHANGE EVENTS

Beyond the normal types of change expected are large-impact events such as mergers and acquisitions (M&A) – both on the client side and the vendor side. These are highly disruptive events, but should be anticipated as the outsourcing market is constantly evolving (e.g., HP acquired EDS in 2008, and ATOS announced the acquisition of Siemens in 2010). Clients can also change their appetite for outsourcing following M&A activity as new executive teams and overlapping deals are brought together into one organisation. Flexibility in a long-term outsourcing deal can be built into a deal with suitable commercial clauses (e.g., the right for a party to terminate early and contract novation clauses).

For example, within two years of JP Morgan signing a seven-year multi-billion-dollar outsourcing deal with IBM in 2002 (Overby S., Backsourcing Pain, 2005), it had merged with another bank and changed its CIO and IT sourcing approach, which resulted in bringing all the outsourced services back in-house. In this situation, the impact of M&A had not been considered, and that, combined with poor transition planning, caused additional cost and significant disruption to key IT programmes.

By contrast, National Savings and Investments in the UK had devised and regularly revisited its "partnership continuity plan" to mitigate key risks that could impact customer service delivery. So when in 2011 ATOS announced it was to acquire their vendor (Siemens, who were 12 years into a 15-year deal), management had prepared a number of contingencies – and with a re-tender only years away decided against their right to bring services back in-house and continued with ATOS as their vendor. In this situation, disruption was minimal since most staff from Siemens simply became ATOS employees.

INNOVATION AND IMPROVEMENT CHANGE

Innovation-driven change is also to be strongly encouraged. A combination of financial incentivization and a positive partnering-style relationship should encourage the vendor to proactively seek opportunities for improvement. Beyond just monitoring the number of innovations proposed, clients should seek contracting mechanisms that give the vendor flexibility and desire to deliver improvements.

PLAN FOR THE END

However, clients should expect and plan for more change at the beginning of a deal than in the final few years. Quite simply, the vendor will want to see a return on investment, and the more years there are left in the deal, the more a vendor is usually prepared to invest. It is not uncommon for vendors to move into a "sweat the assets" mode and invest very little in the final few years of a deal, especially if the client relationship has broken down.

In summary, ensure that provisions for change are built into the deal. Business continuity plans should consider the impact of key events on an outsourcing deal. Both parties should see M&A as a key opportunity to renegotiate terms, or to exit from underperforming deals.

> **TIP:** Every good outsourcing contract must be able to deal with expected changes, such as a variation to scope, pricing or service levels. These are normally dealt with through an agreed change control process, and the deal may include a certain amount of planned change before any pricing renegotiation.

CONCLUSION

The outsourcing industry is now large and mature in many economies, especially the US and Europe. Despite deals being highly varied and covering anything from commodity IT services right through to highly bespoke business processes, the five aspects of a successful outsourcing deal presented in Figure 42 overleaf are relevant to all outsourcing deals.

The correct implementation of these aspects can be difficult to get right, and professional advice should be sought for more complex deals. While risks can be much higher for more complex deals, the rewards can also be significant.

Provided the objectives of both client and vendor are aligned, the deal is structured well, appropriate vendor incentives are in place and the relationship between parties is a positive one, then both client and vendor should be well positioned to reap benefits from the deal.

FIGURE 42: FIVE ASPECTS OF A SUCCESSFUL OUTSOURCING DEAL

Align sourcing requirements to strategy	Ensure that the deal is aligned to the strategic needs of the client
Design the Target Operating Model (TOM)	Design a TOM that sets out the functions and activities retained by the client and the governance of how to manage the vendor
Agree the sourcing strategy	Agree a sourcing strategy that explains exactly what will be outsourced and retained, why and how
Ensure the deal is set up for success	Ensure that the deal is set up for success by building in the right commercial incentives
Be ready for change, and plan for the end	Ensure the deal has flexibility to cater for changes – not only of requirements, but also client strategy, ownership and key personnel

KEY TAKEAWAYS:

1. Align the goals and objectives to support the needs of the organisation
2. Ensure appropriate incentives are in place between the vendor and what the client requires
3. Ensure that provisions for change are built into the deal

4.2 THE RISE OF "NEARSHORING"

AS THE ECONOMIC pressures of long-term recession are still being felt in most of the developed world, offshoring and outsourcing remain key levers for most major corporates in trying to reduce their cost base. But with local political pressure intensifying against sending jobs offshore and many of the typical offshore destinations continuing to experience double-digit rates of inflation, are there any alternatives closer to home that cost-conscious executives can explore? Can Manchester compete with Mumbai?

"Nearshoring", the concept of finding lower-cost locations for business activities on or close to home turf, is not intrinsically a new idea – for decades companies have exploited the lower real-estate costs and lower competition for skills in second-tier cities and regions, locating production and support functions out of the major trading and financial hubs.

However, the newly emerging trend is to see companies using second-tier locations in their home country or very nearby as alternates to the major offshoring centres that have grown up in the last 15–20 years in India, the Philippines, Central and Eastern Europe and more recently in China and South America.

In the UK, major regional cities such as Manchester, Glasgow, Belfast and Newcastle have gained popularity as well as places such as Dublin which, while in a different country, offers many similar characteristics. In the US, states with lower costs of salaries and infrastructure are providing back office services for many major corporations. These include Florida, Texas, Ohio and the Carolinas to name but a few, as well as cities across the border in neighbouring Canada.

As political rhetoric and legislation against offshoring becomes more commonplace, it is likely we will see more and more companies opting to build capabilities closer to home.

Even the Indian vendors are getting in on the act – there have been spates of acquisitions by the big outsourcers of the subcontinent in Europe, the US and further afield, as they realize that to compete in the long term, they will need to be global sourcing providers, not tied to a single geography at the mercy of inflation and spiralling salary costs.

In this section, using the USA and UK as prime examples of the trend, we try to examine the reasons for this shift and consider the factors that should inform decisions on whether to locate (or relocate) services nearshore or offshore. In the following pages, we will examine these arguments for nearshoring:
- Social and political pressures;
- Legislative considerations and restrictions;

- Operational and managerial benefits; and
- The shifting economic arguments.

NEARSHORING POPULARITY INCREASES

Nearshoring is becoming commonplace across a broad range of industries and functions. There are multiple examples of companies bringing or building support functions in nearshore locations across practically every industry sector. This hasn't been confined to companies of a certain scale or type – there are major corporates, niche players and even outsourcing service providers who are also looking to exploit the benefits of siting services closer to their clients.

RECENT SIGNIFICANT EXAMPLES

Banks have led the way - Citibank has developed nearshore operations and IT centres in Florida for its US business, and in Northern Ireland for its European/UK business, in addition to its sites in more typical offshore locations like India, the Philippines and Hungary.

Deutsche Bank has built customer service operations for its Capital Markets clients in Birmingham, UK and has significant operations in Raleigh, North Carolina, as does Credit Suisse.

This approach is particularly common for call centres where the value of cultural alignment in customer-facing staff is of high importance – several UK banks such as NatWest and Halifax have centres in Scotland and the North of England and companies such as Vodafone have sited call centres in areas like Stoke-on-Trent and Greater Manchester.

For those companies that have brought existing offshore operations back onshore, the main driver has been quality of service issues. Even software development companies, the drivers of much offshoring in the 2000s, are opening up onshore centres – with campaigns such as GalaxE's "Outsource to Detroit" (GalaxE Solutions, 2012).

OFFSHORING POPULARITY DECLINES

From the onset of the global recession, the political climate in developed countries began to turn against offshoring even as their corporates sought to leverage it to reduce costs. This has translated into both punitive measures and positive incentives to retain jobs nearer to home.

The language from the White House in particular has been consistently anti-offshoring and outsourcing. This tone has spread to Western Europe too, with politicians in the UK also increasingly defensive about UK jobs going abroad, particularly in the public sector where plans for significant offshoring of NHS IT, and guidelines from the Cabinet Office, stated stringent criteria for any public sector services offshored (Cabinet Office,

FIGURE 43: RECENT EXAMPLES OF COMPANIES DEVELOPING NEARSHORE OPERATIONS (ELIX-IRR ANALYSIS)

COMPANIES	NEARSHORE LOCATION	FUNCTIONS / SERVICES	RATIONALE / DESCRIPTION
Citi	Belfast, N. Ireland Jacksonville, Florida	IT development and support	Government grants, ease of management
Deutsche Bank	Birmingham, UK Raleigh, N. Carolina	Call centre for institutional capital markets clients Operations & IT	Lower cost of real estate and salaries than London Lower cost, time-zone benefits Infrastructure cost, taxation
Aviva	Norwich, UK	Call centres	Quality issues experienced in India
Santander	Glasgow, UK Leicester, UK Liverpool, UK	Call centres	Insourced from WNS in India – service quality
Sky	Newcastle, UK	Call centre	Undisclosed
Vodafone	Manchester, UK	Call centres	Upsell / sales quality
NCR	Columbus, Georgia	Manufacturing	Opened new ATM plant, bringing production back from China
Ford	Avon Lake, Ohio	Manufacturing	Replacing production in Mexico due to tax relief
Caterpillar	Suttner, South Carolina	Manufacturing	Expanding onshore plant capacity
Capita	Various UK sites	Call centres	Acquisition of UK-based call-centre businesses to expand its onshore delivery capabilities
GalaxE Solutions	Detroit, Michigan	Software development	High-quality service
Wipro	Meerbusch, Germany	Datacentre	Acquisition of Citibank datacentre in Germany
HCL	Belfast, N. Ireland	Call centres	Acquisition of BT call centre

2011). It also highlights the public relations element of offshoring, acknowledging that it can stir up hostility due to the loss of UK jobs. It says officials should take instructions from ministers.

THE "STICK"

So far it is only really in the US where punitive measures have been devised to dissuade companies from offshoring, most noticeably with the US "Call Center Worker and Consumer Protection Act" (Overby, 2013). This will make companies who offshore call centres ineligible for any indirect federal loans or loan guarantees for 5 years. The legislation would also require overseas call-centre employees to reveal their location to US consumers and give them the right to be transferred to a call centre in the US.

There are more restrictive measures in place already at a state level – for example, in Arizona any transaction via a call centre where the operator does not disclose their location can be voided, while the Florida senate passed a similar bill requiring disclosure of location in the first 30 seconds and before any personal information is disclosed by the customer.

THE "CARROT"

Beyond these examples of coercive motivation, there is more evidence of the "carrot" approach from governments, with positive incentives being provided at a national and local level to encourage those creating jobs onshore or bringing employment back from overseas, particularly in areas suffering heavily from unemployment.

In the UK, there are multiple tax schemes and grants for the creation of jobs, particularly at a regional level – Northern Ireland in particular has been successful with the grants provided by "Invest NI" which have attracted businesses such as Microsoft and Citibank to set up sites there (Invest Northern Ireland, 2013). The Republic of Ireland is operating similar incentive programmes.

In the US, many states, including Ohio, Utah and Florida, provide significant incentives and tax breaks for companies creating employment. Moreover, at a federal level, a package of tax incentives has been agreed by the White House in discussion with several major US corporations.

Again Barack Obama has been at the forefront of such messages, saying in January 2012, "Ask yourselves what you can do to bring jobs back to your country, and your country will do everything we can to help you succeed."

POTENTIAL OPERATIONAL BENEFITS

Aside from the political environment, there are many potential management and operational benefits of managing support functions closer to home (as indicated in Figure 44 below).

FIGURE 44: POTENTIAL BENEFITS OF NEARSHORING

CULTURAL ALIGNMENT	In particular for customer and front-office facing functions, the importance of cultural alignment is increasingly recognised. While training has gone some way to alleviate such issues, particularly for call centres and so-called "vertical" rather than "horizontal" support functions (i.e. those requiring more in-depth/channel-specific expertise), Santander, BSkyB and New Call Telecom are among the UK companies who have recently moved call-centre operations to low-cost locations in the UK from offshore in India.
LANGUAGE	Language skills are an obvious advantage of onshore/nearshore locations. While this is less of a challenge for English language skills, Western European countries have found language skills scarcer and often of lower quality – for example, German companies have used local delivery solutions or nearby countries such as the Czech Republic and Slovakia.
STAFF RETENTION AND RELOCATION	One benefit of relocating to a nearshore location is the ability to retain or redeploy key staff, at least during transition and stabilization periods. Deutsche Bank experienced this benefit when relocating its capital markets client services operations from London to Birmingham – they were able to retain key management staff which significantly reduced the risk of knowledge loss and reduced time to transfer.
TIME ZONES AND PROXIMITY	Even when key staff are not transferred to the new location, there are significant operational benefits from proximity and working in common time-zones. When Citibank relocated some IT development and support from London to Belfast in Northern Ireland, they found at critical moments in projects or during severe incidents, it was very simple for management from London to go on-site and be more hands-on. Even during normal operating conditions, the location made it much easier for management in head office to spend time there and maintain strong working relationships that would likely have been more difficult and certainly more expensive if the support had been offshore in India/China.
DATA SECURITY	There is much anecdotal evidence of the risks of offshoring data (stolen credit card details, etc.). Though many of these can be effectively managed, risks are generally perceived by regulators and governments to be far lower in nearshore locations. There are several statutes already in force in the US, and many more pending, such as the Health Insurance Portability and Accountability Act ("HIPAA"), in the case of electronically stored or transmitted health-related information, and the Gramm-Leach-Bliley Act ("GLBA") which restricts the movement of data and mandates clear accountability and responsibility for companies operating in offshore locations.

OFFSHORE ARBITRAGE OPPORTUNITIES

The primary motivation for offshoring has historically been the savings from salary arbitrage – while these are still attractive, there are several factors that must be considered that can make the business case far less attractive in the near future.

For many corporations, staff costs are the chief deciding factor in offshoring. However, there are multiple factors that can impact this seemingly attractive arbitrage opportunity. Recent analysis by Elix-IRR, as shown in Figure 45 overleaf, reveals that in some situations this could be diminished by over 40%, and business cases based on this alone should be carefully reviewed.

INFLATION

As unemployment figures remain high in the US and UK, the wage inflation remains low around 2–3%. However, in India salary inflation continues to outstrip basic inflation at around 11–13%. China is in a special situation where the government is keeping consumer price inflation artificially low, but the salary costs are increasing at high single digit rates due to increasing domestic consumption, and according to some sources underlying rates maybe over 20%. Latin-American nations are also typically seeing substantial wage inflation as their economies grow, though in Central and Eastern Europe, inflation has largely stabilized.

ATTRITION

Attrition rates in offshore sites continue to outstrip the mature markets. BPO in India currently suffers from an attrition rate of up to 55% per annum, especially in basic CSR roles. China's is estimated at around 30%. Compared to these figures, US and UK BPO industries enjoy attrition rates of around 20% or lower. Elix-IRR research and analysis shows that attrition costs per resource can be anything between 25% and 40% of the average annual salary cost for one resource (McConnell & Vidal, 2007).

PRODUCTIVITY LOSS

Finally, with offshoring come additional costs of productivity loss, especially in the early stages of the deal. Elix-IRR experience with our clients shows that offshoring operations can cost a company anything from 20–60% in the first 1–3 years depending on the quality and skillset of the resources at the offshore location. A similar relocation to a nearshore location can cost firms something between 5% and 10% if well managed.

FIGURE 45: POTENTIAL CUMULATIVE IMPACT OF FACTORS ON STAFF COST ARBITRAGE (US & UK VS. OFFSHORE LOCATIONS)[2] (ELIX-IRR ANALYSIS)

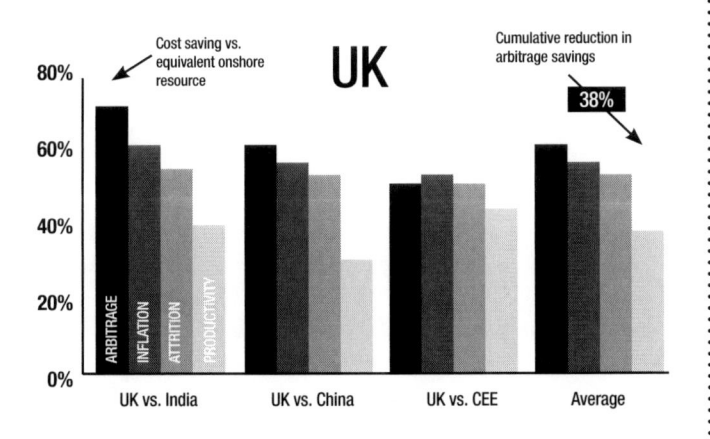

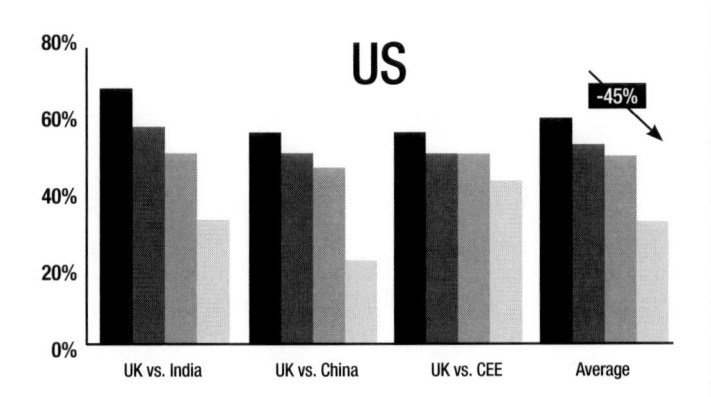

UK

Cost saving vs. equivalent onshore resource

Cumulative reduction in arbitrage savings: 38%

- 2012 Salary arbitrage
- Inflation to 2015 (est.)
- Attrition & training
- Productivity loss

Categories: UK vs. India, UK vs. China, UK vs. CEE, Average

US

-45%

Categories: UK vs. India, UK vs. China, UK vs. CEE, Average

[2] Staff cost comparisons include salary and basic benefits. Arbitrage is based on average across BPO and ITO resources.

REAL-ESTATE COSTS SHOW THAT NEARSHORE LOCATIONS ARE INCREASINGLY COMPETITIVE

The price of real estate is an important cost factor organisations must take into consideration when defining their offshoring strategy. The basic motive to cut costs can well be disrupted in the long term if adequate analysis is not done before choosing the location, especially if significant growth is planned.

RISING COST OF OFFSHORE REAL ESTATE

Such has become the case with cities like Mumbai in India and Guangzhou in China. The shortage of supply for office space and emergence of these cities as global economic centres in their own right has seen dramatic price increases in the last decade. Couple this with the property crisis in many parts of the US and Western Europe where years of boom saw an overstock when recession hit and now Tier 2 locations in the UK and US look attractively priced, certainly compared with Tier 1 locations in the offshore countries, and this trend looks set to continue for several years. According to real-estate services firm Jones Lang LaSalle, there was a record take-up of office spaces in offshore locations in 2011, with the trend continuing into 2012. Rents and capital values are also still rising in most markets. The good old days where one would offshore operations in order to capitalize on the arbitrage opportunities provided by the real-estate costs of the emerging markets are numbered, certainly unless you look further afield at so-called "Tier 2" city locations.

INCREASING NEARSHORE APPEAL

Comparatively, prices for office space look attractive in several domestic cities within the US and UK. Recent studies show that office space prices have gone down considerably in regional UK cities like Birmingham, Manchester, Newcastle, Belfast and Cardiff. The average serviced office rents (per person) in 2012 stood at £125 per month in Birmingham and £82 in Manchester, down from 2011 highs of £159 and £96 per person per month (around 20%) respectively (Jones Lang LaSalle, 2012; Cushman & Wakefield, 2012). Such trends are also true for US cities like Jacksonville, Raleigh, Detroit and Atlanta where office space is both plentiful and cheap, compared to Tier 1 cities in low-cost emerging markets.

Figure 46 below shows how prime rent of office spaces per month in traditional outsourcing locations within Asia, CEE and Latin America is now comparable to that in Tier 2 domestic locations within the US or UK. Figure 47 forecasts the movement of the prime rents for the same cities for the coming years. The rents in traditional offshore locations are typically growing, whereas the same in domestic cities within the US or UK are stabilizing.

FIGURE 46: 2011 OFFICE SPACE PRIME RENTS FOR SAMPLE OFFSHORE AND NEARSHORE LOCATIONS (USD/SQFT./MONTH) (ELIX-IRR ANALYSIS; JONES LANG LASALLE VARIOUS REPORTS; CUSHMAN & WAKEFIELD, 2012)

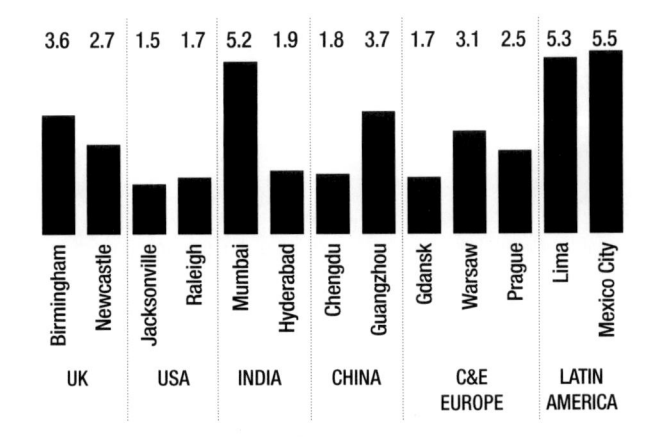

UK		USA		INDIA		CHINA		C&E EUROPE			LATIN AMERICA	
Birmingham	Newcastle	Jacksonville	Raleigh	Mumbai	Hyderabad	Chengdu	Guangzhou	Gdansk	Warsaw	Prague	Lima	Mexico City
3.6	2.7	1.5	1.7	5.2	1.9	1.8	3.7	1.7	3.1	2.5	5.3	5.5

FIGURE 47: FORECAST FOR RENTAL PRICE MOVEMENT, 2012 ONWARDS (ELIX-IRR ANALYSIS; JONES LANG LASALLE VARIOUS REPORTS; CUSHMAN & WAKEFIELD, 2012)

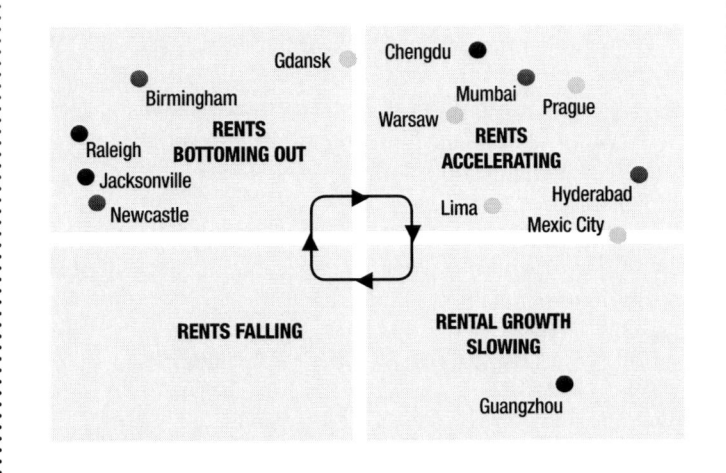

RENTS BOTTOMING OUT: Gdansk, Birmingham, Raleigh, Jacksonville, Newcastle

RENTS ACCELERATING: Chengdu, Mumbai, Prague, Warsaw, Lima, Hyderabad, Mexic City

RENTS FALLING

RENTAL GROWTH SLOWING: Guangzhou

HIDDEN COSTS

Unforeseen costs in set-up and ongoing management can also affect offshoring business cases.

The bargain-basement labour rates that tempt firms to ship operations to India or China tell only a fraction of the story about cost savings related to offshoring. In reality, there are a lot more hidden costs involved in this process. Indeed, there are substantial savings, but depending on the methods adopted and sourcing decisions made, it can take years of effort and large up-front investment to reach that optimum cost-saving phase.

These costs can be broadly categorized into up-front capital investments and one-off project spend required to manage transition, and ongoing management expenses necessary for proper integration.

The cost of transition management can vary significantly depending on scale and complexity, but we estimate between 3% and 5% of the total deal value. The costs of this transition phase are the costs for licensing before setting up at the offshore location, costs for setting up an infrastructure and communications at the location, costs of internal resources assigned for project management and costs of training resources from offshore locations to iron out the knowledge gap. Additionally, the process demands a lot of international travel, so there are ancillary expenses like visa costs, travelling expenses and allowances. Even more significantly, during this transition there may be significant expenditure in severance and redeployment costs resulting from layoffs.

The offshoring and/or outsourcing of services does entail additional overhead for effective management – retained onshore management staff, vendor and service management, auditing the processes, additional training and travel expenses to name a few – and can account for up to 5–8% of the total deal value.

In totality, these expenses may well be between 10% and 15% of the total deal value, or more if the scale of offshore implementation is relatively small (say, sub-100 FTEs). Hence, in those situations nearshoring becomes an attractive option. The proportion of these expenses reduces considerably on selecting the right location, preferably a city closer to the home country.

Figure 48 overleaf shows the estimated value of the capital and operational investments as a percentage of the total deal value and standard types of costs involved during the deal.

CONCLUSION – NEARSHORING AS PART OF A BALANCED SOURCING STRATEGY

Offshoring has been an excellent and proven management tool for improving cost, productivity and quality. However, with changes in the

FIGURE 48: TRANSITION AND ONGOING MANAGEMENT COSTS AS A PERCENTAGE OF TOTAL OFFSHORING DEAL VALUE (SOURCE: ELIX-IRR ANALYSIS; OVERBY S., 2003)

Ongoing Management Costs

- Retained management team and vendor managers
- Auditing
- Invoicing and financial management
- Travel and visa costs
- Additional infrastructure and technology licensing Opex

Pie chart segments: 5 – 8%, 3 – 5%, Total deal value

Transition Costs

- Capital costs of licensing, telecoms and other technology infrastructure
- Training
- Recruiting
- Travel, visas and other knowledge transfer costs
- Severance, and staff incentive programmes

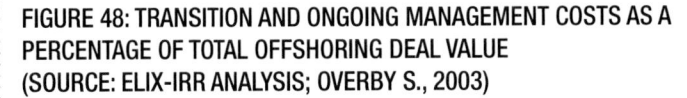

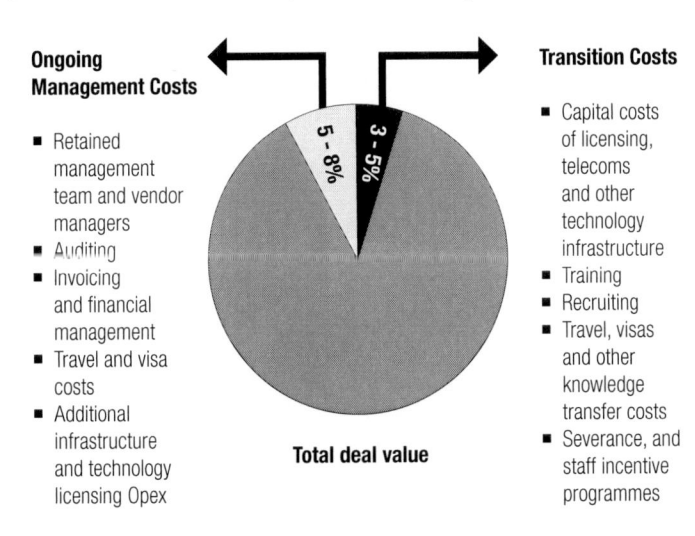

macroeconomic factors that made offshoring attractive, organisations need to reconfirm their strategy. As well as the expansion of potential offshoring destinations into Tier 2 cities and new regions like South America and Africa, there are many attractive nearshore locations for countries like the US, UK, Germany, France and Japan which will have an increasing role to play in the global sourcing landscape.

That is not to suggest that offshoring will disappear as a viable strategy; many of the offshoring risks and issues highlighted in this chapter can be overcome, and indeed, many companies are now using offshore outsourced capabilities to enhance their skills and productivity beyond unit cost improvements. Rather, a consideration of nearshore delivery should be part of any location and/or sourcing decisions and increasingly, we believe, companies must diversify their portfolio of nearshore and offshore operations in order to minimize economic, operational, geopolitical and cultural risk, while optimizing competencies and costs. Realizing the potential of having a local presence, service providers too are expanding their footprint and establishing operations across the globe. Firms should capitalize on these moves to create strategic alliances with service providers with a flexible balance of offshore, nearshore and onsite delivery capabilities.

KEY TAKEAWAYS:

1. "Nearshoring" is the concept of finding lower-cost locations for business activities on or close to home turf
2. This approach is particularly common for call centres where the value of cultural alignment in customer-facing staff is of high importance
3. Companies must diversify their portfolio of nearshore and offshore operations in order to minimize economic, operational, geopolitical and cultural risk, while optimizing competencies and costs

4.3 RETAIL IT SOURCING TODAY

IT OUTSOURCING IN RETAIL UNCOMMON COMPARED TO OTHER INDUSTRIES

THE USE OF THIRD-PARTY IT SUPPLIERS to deliver hardware, software and services is widespread within the retail sector, as it is in other industries. However, large transformational outsourcing deals are not as prevalent within retail as in other industries, such as financial services and the public sector.

This section explores why this may be so, and how the need for innovation in the age of internet shopping may drive change in the IT sourcing landscape for retail.

Analysis shows that only 2% of the $127.2bn in global IT outsourcing (ITO)/Business Process Outsourcing (BPO) spend between Q2 2011 to Q2 2012 can be attributed to the retail industry (see Figure 49).

Large-scale outsourcing has not been popular in retail, perhaps due to perceptions that major transformational deals are too risky or do not deliver value, with the Sainsbury's Accenture deal often cited as an example (ComputerWeekly, 2005).

A stronger rationale may be the desire that many retailers, constantly challenged by uncertain short-term demand, have to maintain maximum flexibility. This conflicts with IT vendors' desire to secure longer-term and more valuable deals. However, as outsourcing has matured as an industry, flexibility can now be more successfully built into outsourcing contracts, when compared to earlier "first-generation" deals.

The benefits that ITO deals can offer are slowly being recognised by some retailers. A 2011 TPI study, quoted by Computerweekly.com, showed that EMEA retail outsourcing grew by 75% in 2011 alone (Flinders, 2011).

POTENTIAL BENEFITS OF IT OUTSOURCING:
- **COST REDUCTION** – while retailers typically have narrow margins and low levels of IT spend compared to other industries, ITO can reduce costs even further through labour arbitrage, consolidated sourcing and the delivery of faster business transformation;
- **FLEXIBILITY** – given the right contract structures and engagement model, flexibility can help to optimize the IT services delivered to the rapidly changing demands of a multichannel retail business;
- **INNOVATION AND NEW CAPABILITIES** – getting access to the right skills and experience, especially in areas of innovation (e.g., multichannel

or mobile payments), and the ability to leverage investments in the latest technologies (e.g., near field communications);
- **IMPROVED QUALITY OF SERVICES** – using "best in the market" IT services may deliver better-quality solutions compared to an in-house solution, which in turn may result in better business outcomes;
- **FASTER DELIVERY OF IT CHANGE** – sourcing the right capability and capacity will enable faster delivery of business outcomes; and
- **RISK REDUCTION** – getting the deal right in the first place, and then implementing a robust governance structure for managing the vendor performance, should lead to a reduction of IT-related risks to the business.

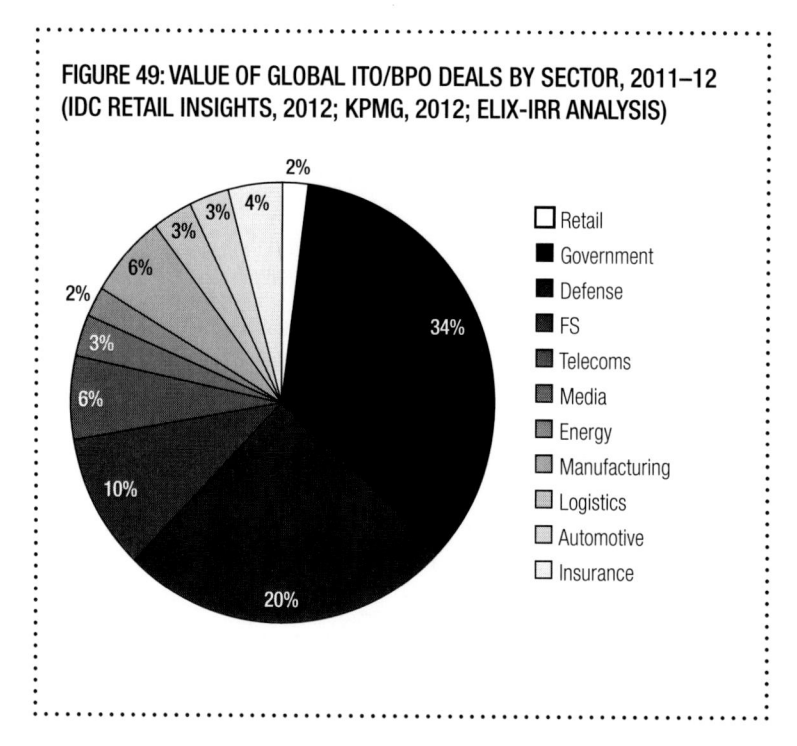

FIGURE 49: VALUE OF GLOBAL ITO/BPO DEALS BY SECTOR, 2011–12 (IDC RETAIL INSIGHTS, 2012; KPMG, 2012; ELIX-IRR ANALYSIS)

Sector	%
Retail	34%
Government	20%
Defense	10%
FS	6%
Telecoms	3%
Media	2%
Energy	6%
Manufacturing	3%
Logistics	3%
Automotive	4%
Insurance	2%

WHAT TYPES OF DEALS ARE RETAILERS SIGNING?
1. WIDE-SCOPE IT OUTSOURCING DEALS ARE RARE

There are few examples of outsourcing deals in retail where all IT services are provided by a single vendor. More usual is the acquisition of specific IT services and the use of third parties for labour augmentation. A recent report from Martec International showed that only 5% of the leading 100 retailers have outsourced their entire IT function (Martec International, 2011). This is supported by our own review of IT sourcing deals in retail, which indicates that many IT services are likely to be delivered by an in-house team, though perhaps with the support of contractors and commodity IT suppliers. Application Maintenance and Support and Data Centres are the two most commonly outsourced IT services.

Notable examples of companies that have agreed wide-scope IT sourcing deals include:
- Aurora (outsourced all IT to Retail Assist);
- DSG (to HCL, signed in 2006 and extended to 2013);
- Matalan (to Capgemini, 6-year deal signed in 2007); and
- Phones 4 U (to TCS, in a 2008 deal).

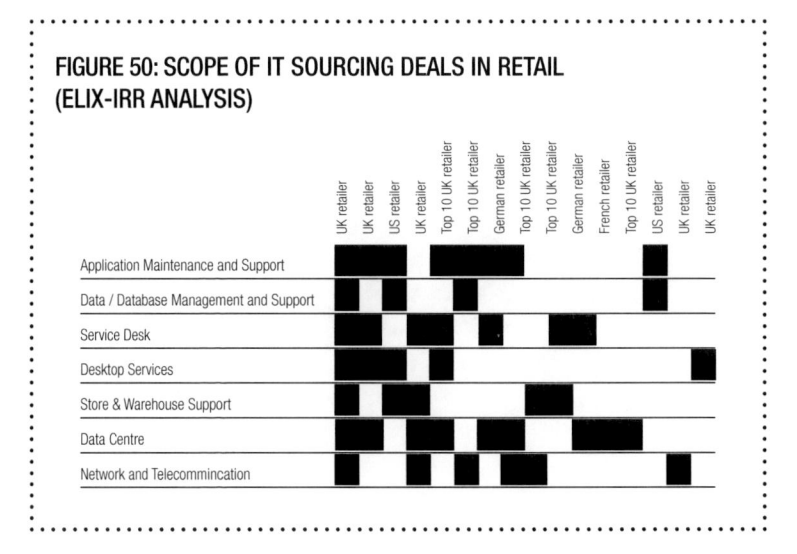

FIGURE 50: SCOPE OF IT SOURCING DEALS IN RETAIL (ELIX-IRR ANALYSIS)

Service	UK retailer	UK retailer	US retailer	UK retailer	Top 10 UK retailer	Top 10 UK retailer	German retailer	Top 10 UK retailer	Top 10 UK retailer	German retailer	French retailer	Top 10 UK retailer	US retailer	UK retailer	UK retailer
Application Maintenance and Support	■				■	■	■						■		
Data / Database Management and Support		■							■				■		
Service Desk		■					■	■							
Desktop Services	■	■													■
Store & Warehouse Support	■	■						■							
Data Centre	■			■		■						■			
Network and Telecommincation		■										■	■		

EUROPEAN INFRASTRUCTURE OUTSOURCING DOMINATES

At $9.7bn the European ITO market is nearly 3.5 times the size of the American market, and over 12 times larger than the Asian Pacific ITO market (see Figure 51 overleaf).

Most "business as usual" ITO services focus on IT infrastructure domains, which include Data Centre, Network and Telecommunications, and Desktop IT Services. This is not surprising as these are mature markets dealing in IT services that may be considered commodities. These are services that are easily understood, bought and sold often, and where competitive forces are strong, meaning prices can be driven down.

This is not the case for more complex IT areas such as systems integration and large-scale IT-led transformation – these deals are harder to craft and more challenging to agree. This is especially true among retailers where business demand for IT fluctuates, and may not be aligned across different operating companies.

While the market for ITO in retail is small compared to other industries, retailers that have not yet outsourced significant aspects of their infrastructure may be missing some great opportunities to reduce cost, gain flexibility and new capability, and reduce risk.

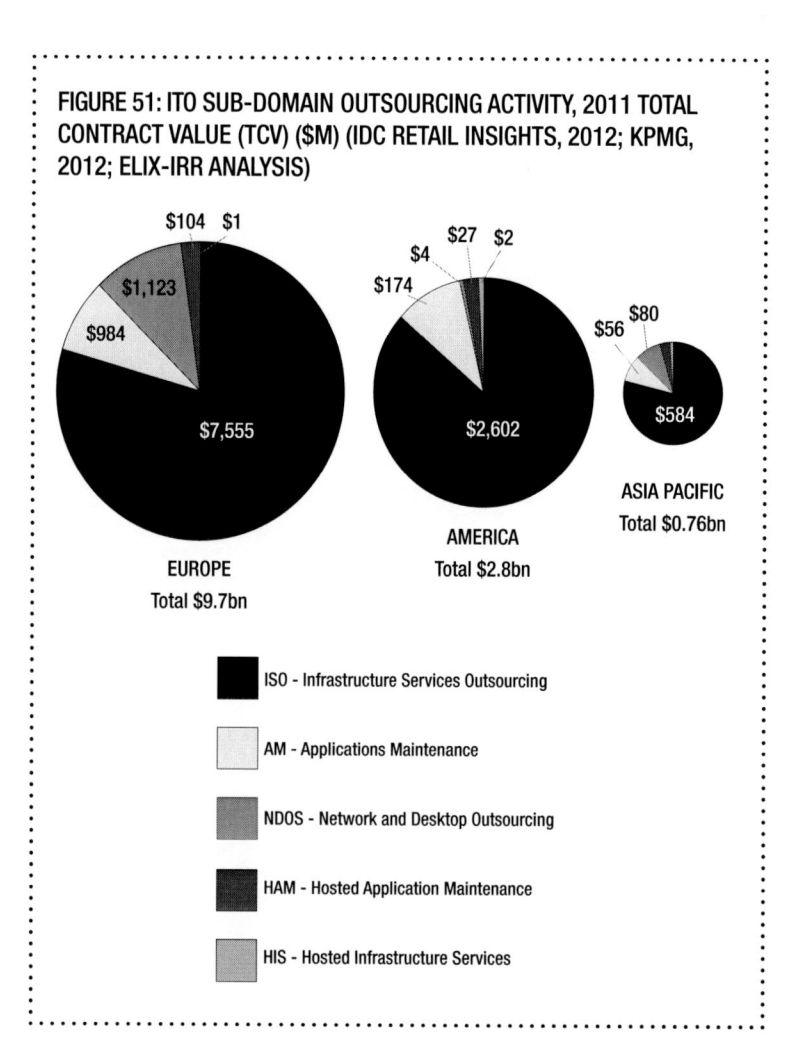

FIGURE 51: ITO SUB-DOMAIN OUTSOURCING ACTIVITY, 2011 TOTAL CONTRACT VALUE (TCV) ($M) (IDC RETAIL INSIGHTS, 2012; KPMG, 2012; ELIX-IRR ANALYSIS)

EUROPE
Total $9.7bn
- $7,555
- $1,123
- $984
- $104
- $1

AMERICA
Total $2.8bn
- $2,602
- $174
- $27
- $4
- $2

ASIA PACIFIC
Total $0.76bn
- $584
- $80
- $56

- ISO - Infrastructure Services Outsourcing
- AM - Applications Maintenance
- NDOS - Network and Desktop Outsourcing
- HAM - Hosted Application Maintenance
- HIS - Hosted Infrastructure Services

RETAIL TRENDS AND THEIR IMPACT ON TECHNOLOGY AND IT SOURCING

Changing consumer buying habits, the growth of internet-only retailers, economic pressures and the availability of new technology services are changing the sourcing landscape for retail information technology. The following table (Figure 52) describes some of the key trends in this space.

FIGURE 52: IMPACT OF MAJOR RETAIL TRENDS ON TECHNOLOGY AND IT SOURCING

RETAIL TREND	NEARSHORE LOCATION

The Internet makes it more difficult for retailers to differentiate their offer	▪ The internet reduces differentiation based on:
	  ▪ Range (you can buy anything online)
	  ▪ Location (you can buy from anywhere and have items delivered to you)
	  ▪ Price (comparison websites expose non-competitive offers which can then be ignored)
	▪ Innovation through technology enables retailers to differentiate their offer (e.g., click and collect for convenience, or wireless POS terminals with email receipts for speedy transactions). Thus having access to innovation from IT vendors can put retailers ahead of the competition

Multichannel	▪ The need to offer an integrated customer experience across many channels (e.g., store, online, telephone, kiosks and smartphone apps) will stretch the capabilities of IT departments ▪ Integration of multiple solutions from different providers will be required to develop a cohesive multichannel experience; retailers could take on responsibility for systems integration (SI) or could engage an SI partner with deeper e-business capabilities ▪ Once the solution is built, both internal users and customers will need to be supported, and this support may be best provided by the vendors that have experience of multichannel solutions
Internet technologies drive new skill requirements	▪ Responding to the threat of online retailers, traditional retailers are investing in their own e-commerce solutions ▪ With the focus on multichannel solutions, there is an increasing requirement for internet-centric skills, which some retailers may lack ▪ The capability and capacity required to build and deploy these solutions rapidly can be provided by large IT vendors more quickly and flexibly, compared to up-skilling and deploying internal resources

Economic pressures	▪ A period of weakened consumer demand has resulted in reduced revenues, which in turn has driven a focus on cost reduction ▪ Since IT is generally seen as a "cost centre" that does not deliver revenue, retail CIOs are under increasing pressure to reduce costs (while still delivering innovation for the business!) ▪ Larger IT sourcing deals provide opportunities to reduce in-year costs through labour arbitrage, economies of scale, process efficiency and automation, and financial engineering
Cloud and managed services	▪ Cloud-based/hosted services are increasingly accepted across a range of industries as concerns regarding data security and continuity are addressed ▪ Utility-based pricing models where full managed services are delivered based on consumption offer scalability, flexibility and predictability ▪ Business users are able to acquire hosted solutions (e.g., data analytics) directly from "full-service vendors", with minimal involvement from IT. However, IT will be left with the challenge of integrating systems and providing support
Data-driven customer insight	▪ Many retailers now capture and hold vast amounts of data on inventory information, product sales trends and customer buying habits ▪ Data analytics can improve profitability, but requires new data management, data mining and business intelligence capabilities ▪ Customer insight capabilities, which combine retailers' own data sets with many other data sets, are increasingly available from the market

CONCLUSION
- Effective IT sourcing can deliver benefits to retailers, including cost and risk reduction, innovation and flexibility – all of which will help to deliver a better bottom line.
- Many traditional retailers currently relying on in-house IT teams supplemented by contractors may have an inefficient delivery model that is not fit for purpose in the fast-moving world of multichannel. They may be missing an opportunity to realize IT cost savings through smarter IT sourcing.
- Retailers must innovate to differentiate their offerings, and should lean on the expertise of technology vendors to support their innovation agenda. They should acquire commodity IT services (such as desktop computing and infrastructure) as managed services from vendors, leaving their precious internal resources to focus on

what makes a difference – building the right customer experience.

If the organisation has a complicated supplier landscape with many IT suppliers and contracts, struggles to deliver IT-led customer improvement quickly or largely delivers IT services with an in-house team supplemented by contractors, then perhaps it is time to think about the IT sourcing strategy.

KEY TAKEAWAYS:

1. Retailers may be missing an opportunity to realize cost savings through smarter IT sourcing
2. There are a growing number of opportunities to leverage the expertise of technology vendors, and to acquire commodity IT services
3. Internal resources should be focused on the true value-add capabilities

4.4 TO RFP OR NOT TO RFP? USING COLLABORATIVE SOURCING AS A VIABLE ALTERNATIVE

WHEN EMBARKING UPON an outsourcing journey, most advisors in the market today will suggest putting the bid out to tender amongst suppliers. Requests for Proposal (RFPs) can be an efficient way of comparing vendors in terms of commercials and agreement to contractual terms. But they are also an efficient way of making sourcing advisors healthy margins, delaying the business case by up to a year, and disconnecting the solution from the original strategic intent. Whilst the RFP process certainly has a time and a place, it should not be the default journey companies embark upon. Indeed, often it is simply the wrong commercial decision.

There are alternative approaches to sourcing that may be more appropriate and can help to speed up the delivery of desired benefits. In this chapter, we explore one such alternative – Elix-IRR's innovative Collaborative Solutioning methodology, which encourages iterative solution development between the client and potential suppliers.

THE RFP DILEMMA

There is a school of thought that teaches that outsourcing deals should always be put out to tender in order to leverage a company's negotiating ability and purchasing power with suppliers and thereby obtain the most competitive bid. This school of thought currently has a plethora of followers, and is very much in vogue in today's world. As with most popular things, RFPs are in place because people have used them before and they have been successful. If the RFP process did not work over time, RFPs would not exist – simple Darwinism. However, just because they have "worked" and produced a "successful" outcome, it does not necessarily mean it is an optimal outcome – in a commercial, strategic or operational sense. An analogy to make this point might be as follows. Motorbikes are popular. They are used in vast quantities and many people swear by them. However, whilst it would be possible to get from Land's End to John O'Groats on a motorbike successfully, and the motorbike will (hopefully!) work, it is not necessarily the optimal way of doing it. There are other modes of transport that do it more quickly, cheaply, easily and efficiently. Motorbikes are certainly an option, but not necessarily the optimal choice in this instance.

The same applies with RFPs – they certainly work and are successful in navigating a client along an outsourcing journey, but they are not necessarily the optimal choice in each instance. The assertion of this section is that perhaps client executives are too readily donning their motorbike helmets when beginning the outsourcing journey, before thoroughly thinking through the steps involved. And here's why.

THE BENEFITS OF AN RFP

It is well documented that the RFP process has particular benefits. Typing "RFP Benefits" into Google produces the Wikipedia entry for "Request for Proposal" as the top hit. Within this article, the key benefits are as follows:

- It informs suppliers that your company is looking to procure and encourages them to make their best effort;
- It requires the company to specify what it proposes to purchase. If the requirements analysis has been prepared properly, it can be incorporated quite easily into the Request document;
- It alerts suppliers that the selection process is competitive;
- It allows for wide distribution and response;
- It ensures that suppliers respond factually to the identified requirements; and
- By following a structured evaluation and selection procedure, an organisation can demonstrate impartiality – a crucial factor in public sector procurement.

This is all very useful and does not include anything too contentious, but perhaps is a little incomplete. Further benefits include the fact that by asking for a standard response, it is very easy to compare responses from different suppliers. This is a good way of ensuring that clients (and advisors) are comparing "apples to apples", in terms of both the solution and the business case, and thus empowering a considered decision. The RFP process should also ensure that suppliers submit their most competitive bids in full knowledge that it is a competition, and that if they do not submit a price and terms that have a chance of winning the deal, they will not be invited to the next round of submissions.

This list of benefits is by no means exhaustive, but should hopefully acknowledge that there are certain benefits associated with the RFP process. But to cut to the chase, these tend to be outweighed by the disadvantages.

LOWEST PRICE + GOOD COMMERCIAL TERMS = BEST DEAL

It is well documented that the RFP process can often result in the selection of a supplier for the wrong reasons. For example, a supplier might be discounted in the RFP process for submitting too many mark-ups to original documentation, or for being too expensive. However, often the suppliers who are chosen due to a perceived "ease of working together" (i.e. few mark-ups) will change control themselves out of the original agreements. This is a common trait amongst certain suppliers, and it is important that a client's sourcing advisor can recognize the likely candidates. The net effect is that delivery and associated savings end up being a world away from where the client's vision and business case were at the outset. Further, those suppliers chosen on having the cheapest solution will often be delivering to such a tight margin that the engagement has a lack of senior attention within the supplier, resulting in second-rate delivery and a client team that is regarded internally by the supplier as the "B" team. The "A" team is reserved for highly profitable, mainstream clients. Again, something the client's advisor should know as a matter of course.

Another characteristic of the RFP process is that it often results in the selection of a supplier whose capabilities were well known at the outset – essentially, the RFP process is used to facilitate a foregone conclusion and merely adhere to internal procurement policies. Worse, sourcing advisors often already have an idea of a supplier in mind (an effect of having a limited knowledge of the supplier environment), and therefore use the RFP process to make a lot of money to help make a decision that has already been made. They will then steer their client towards making the same decision – wasting valuable time and money in the process. This leads to possible friction for the client project lead with the project sponsor, who will want to know why there has been a delay choosing a supplier and why the promises made in the business case have not been kept. Reduced time to full benefits realization is certainly not something that is facilitated by the RFP process.

One interesting point here is that suppliers, by nature of the RFP process, do not get paid for the time they spend responding to them. Therefore, the more RFP processes suppliers respond to, and the longer they take, the more money they have to recover by baking this cost into the solution price curve. This clearly hurts the business case. Suppliers are waking up to this fact too, and some would rather not respond to an RFP unless they are of a certain size, because the time it takes to earn an acceptable return on their investment outweighs the lifetime value of the deal. They instead prefer to concentrate on the high-value, high-return deals, even if this means responding to an RFP.

ONE-WAY STREET?

Perhaps even more worryingly than this, the RFP process often leads the selection process down a path that ends up purely concentrating on price, process and terms. The RFP is essentially a draft contract that is written by people who often have no operational experience of actually outsourcing – from both the client perspective and the advisors themselves. They are writing from a point of view where they have read in books "what good looks like", and try to force-fit this "best practice" into a situation that is not necessarily receptive to it. RFPs need to be written by people who know how outsourcing engagements work on the ground, who have "been there, done that", who recognize the interactions and hand-offs between operations and processes, who fully understand the commercial risk associated with large engagements, and who understand how to spread this risk fairly amongst the parties involved. They should not be drawn up (if they are drawn up at all!) by clever people who have clever thoughts, but unfortunately do not have clever experience. Doing this loses sight of key strategic and commercial levers like value creation, vision, strategy, transparency and governance.

The "right" advisor will be able to keep all these aspects at the forefront of all supplier discussions, whether within the RFP process or not. The traditional RFP argument states that the RFP process will get the best price and contractual terms. However, this is actually a reflection on the advisor – the "right" advisor will ensure this whatever the tender process, as well as securing optimal agreements on the other aspects of outsourcing engagements.

The final argument as to why the RFP process is not necessarily the correct decision revolves around relationships. The relationship that a client has with their supplier is essentially a marriage – both parties are inextricably linked together, live together every day, and the better they get on without hurting the other (emotionally, commercially, politically or rationally), the better the relationship will be in the future. The RFP process is analogous to those reality dating programmes you find on TV. One person is presented with 8–10 potential partners, and these potential partners spend the next 12 weeks each trying to persuade the person in question that they are the right partner for them and that life with them would be amazing. Week after week, the potential suitors are whittled down to one, having had to present a case each week for why they should be kept in the competition. Now, once the partner has been chosen, the dynamic changes between the chosen partner and the main star of the show, given the footing that they started from. No-one likes to be compared for 12 weeks to others and to be selected in a "close-call" at the end – emotions, politics, rationality, etc. will all kick in.

WRONG FOOT FORWARD?

Whilst this analogy might be slightly tenuous, the point is that RFP processes start relationships off on the wrong footing. They are secretive, often confrontational, and in terms of how to start a relationship, against good practice. They also do not promote much interaction – time would be far better spent working day-to-day with your sourcing advisor and one chosen supplier, strengthening the vision together, improving the business case, etc., rather than a prolonged, protracted "courting" period. There will obviously need to be a selection procedure to choose the "right" supplier, but there is no need for a several month-long RFP process to do this. Working closely with your sourcing advisor, looking at the strategic intent for outsourcing, the scope of work and the desired business case will enable the right supplier to be asked to submit thoughts/offers/proposals in far less time than an official RFP.

COLLABORATIVE SOLUTIONING EXPLAINED

A more agile approach for completing the outsourcing journey can not only help to reach the destination quicker, but also result in a more optimal long-term outcome by laying a solid foundation for the client-vendor relationship from the start.

Elix-IRR have developed an alternative to the traditional RFP process called Collaborative Solutioning, whose effectiveness we have tested through a variety of client engagements. Collaborative Solutioning is a highly interactive approach, which relies on repeated face-to-face interaction through a series of structured workshops. In the course of these interactions, vendors present their solutions and the client has the opportunity to assess not only the merits of each solution, but also the cultural fit of their potential partners.

Figure 53, right, presents an overview of the different elements of Elix-IRR's Collaborative Solutioning methodology.

Adopting an alternative process, such as Collaborative Solutioning, allows the client to engage with potential suppliers on an ongoing basis and focus on fleshing out the desired solution, testing the compatibility between supplier and client in the process. Additionally, it condenses the time required to select the preferred supplier, thereby reducing the cost of the process and accelerating the time before the benefits of the project begin to accrue. Figure 54 overleaf summarizes the key differences between the traditional RFP process and Collaborative Solutioning.

TRUSTED ADVISOR IS KEY

Obtaining a trusted sourcing advisor is fundamental to a successful outsourcing journey. The client's advisor should have experience and

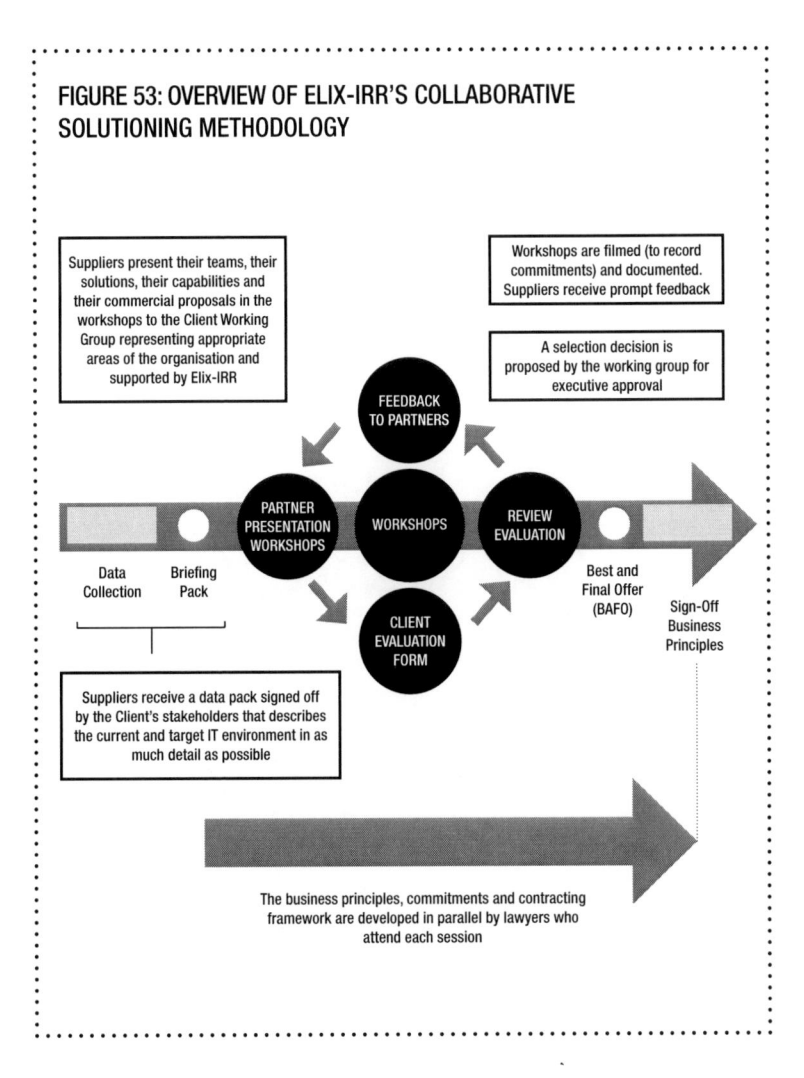

FIGURE 53: OVERVIEW OF ELIX-IRR'S COLLABORATIVE SOLUTIONING METHODOLOGY

Suppliers present their teams, their solutions, their capabilities and their commercial proposals in the workshops to the Client Working Group representing appropriate areas of the organisation and supported by Elix-IRR

Workshops are filmed (to record commitments) and documented. Suppliers receive prompt feedback

A selection decision is proposed by the working group for executive approval

Data Collection — Briefing Pack — PARTNER PRESENTATION WORKSHOPS — WORKSHOPS — FEEDBACK TO PARTNERS — CLIENT EVALUATION FORM — REVIEW EVALUATION — Best and Final Offer (BAFO) — Sign-Off Business Principles

Suppliers receive a data pack signed off by the Client's stakeholders that describes the current and target IT environment in as much detail as possible

The business principles, commitments and contracting framework are developed in parallel by lawyers who attend each session

---

deep understanding of all aspects of an outsourcing journey – buying, selling, advising and legal considerations. They need to have "been there, done that". Without these four aspects, the contracts signed with the chosen supplier will almost certainly be suboptimal.

RFPs do work in certain situations, especially for smaller deals, but be mindful of all the negative points they bring. Ensure the organisation's advisor is not using the RFP process as a way for them to make a few months of healthy consulting fees. The "right" advisor will not need to do this. Indeed, they will not want to.

Alternative approaches do exist. Elix-IRR's Collaborative Solutioning methodology is an example of an alternative that has been successfully deployed by a number of clients, driving towards the realization of desired benefits in a far more optimal manner than the traditional RFP.

A final word. Ensure that the business works closely with its advisor to shape the initial vision and business case. The reasons to outsource need to be strong and make commercial sense. If they do not, then the decision to outsource is incorrect. The "right" advisor will look to uncover the intent in the outsourcing decision, and if the decision does not make sense for the business, they will not be afraid to advise against it, even if this results in much less fees for the advisor in question. These are the traits of an advisor that a client can trust.

FIGURE 54: COMPARISON OF RFP AND COLLABORATIVE SOLUTIONING

COLLABORATIVE SOLUTIONING APPROACH	TRADITIONAL RFP
■ More open-ended and flexible approach, leaving room for creativity	■ Highly prescriptive in nature
■ No requirement to write detailed specifications for solution and scope at the outset – focus on collaborative way of working between the client and partner to develop joint solution	■ Difficult to write detailed specifications for business problem that requires complex solution
■ Encourages innovative thinking to shape the best outcome for the client	■ Gives partners a "list-based" documentation of RFP requirements which can limit solutions
■ Allows for better communication of requirements to potential partners during workshops	■ Difficult to accurately communicate requirements to potential partners
■ Continuous evaluation of partners against weighted criteria and communication to partners allows them to incorporate the feedback and improve their solution, creating a more bespoke outcome	■ No feedback is provided to partners, therefore, they are unable to adjust the solution to fit the requirements
■ Through the workshops, client is able to assess the cultural fit and build relationships with potential partner organisations	■ Interaction with potential partners is limited to formal mechanisms i.e. submissions of responses
■ Contract principles are developed in parallel, thereby accelerating the contracting process	■ Contract principles are normally developed after the RFP response is received and partner is selected, thus making this a longer process

KEY TAKEAWAYS:

1. The RFP process has a time and a place, but it should not be the default journey companies embark upon
2. In many cases, defaulting to the RFP process presents a suboptimal commercial decision
3. Alternatives, such as Collaborative Solutioning, can deliver desired benefits in a more optimal manner than more traditional approaches

ELIX-IRR'S SENIOR TEAM

WITH OVER 60 practitioners and growing rapidly, Elix-IRR's diversity is one of its key strengths. Our people range from graduates to senior retail industry professionals, from over 14 countries, and they are able to advise our clients in 15 languages. This allows us to provide advice to our clients that truly transcends capabilities and geographies.

Below we introduce Elix-IRR's senior team who contributed towards the creation of the chapters presented in this book.

1. RETAIL STRATEGY

BRIAN KALMS leads the Elix-IRR Retail practice. He typically consults on key stores, multichannel and retail supply chain initiatives. He has worked with many of the UK's leading retailers and across most sectors (including food, non-food, speciality and convenience) as well as leading teams in South Africa, China and America.

TOBY BYRNE leads our multichannel work. He has experience working with retail and consumer clients with a focus on digital change and the development of multichannel operating models. He has recently completed projects to assist a major global retailer in the design and implementation of a multichannel operating model and the digital transformation of a leading UK home and electrical retailer.

OLI FREESTONE specializes in working with retail and consumer clients with a focus on digital transformation and multichannel technology. Recent projects include designing a digital learning experience for a large UK retailer, developing a Target Operating Model for a leading department store chain and the development and delivery of a digital strategy and transformation programme for an international publisher.

EÓIN O'GORMAN is an expert in digital strategy, industry disruption and innovation. Over the last 5 years, he has led numerous consulting engagements addressing the impact of "digital" on businesses and industries, whether the positive impact of exploring innovative growth or the negative impact of traditional business models losing relevance.

2. DRIVING EFFICIENCY AND INSIGHT

BARRY LEWIS has over 40 years of line operations experience at various Tier 1 global investment banks, the past 20 years at MD level. His specialities include operations risk and operations transformation. Prior to joining Elix-IRR, Barry was Global Head of Operations Shared Services at Credit Suisse.

JILL ROSS has many years' retail industry and consulting experience, having previously held positions in industry (including Commercial Manager at Marks & Spencer) and partnered with leading UK and international retailers to define and deliver change. Recent assignments include designing and delivering the global operating model for a leading luxury retailer and evolving the multichannel capabilities of a UK supermarket.

AVIS DARZINS has a strong background in retail operational transformation, and has led multiple optimization initiatives, mergers & acquisitions and international expansions. She was a partner in a management consulting practice, and most recently was Director of Business Transformation at BSkyB where she established and led a team of transformation experts. She is a board member of Retail Trust.

JOE DALL has over 20 years of industry and consulting experience, and specializes in strategy, technology-enabled transformation and sourcing. Joe has strong cross-sector experience gained from several technology transformation projects. Joe's breadth of experience also includes recent IT operating model design and implementation for FTSE100 retailers.

3. ORGANIZING FOR SUCCESS

STEPHEN NEWTON is Elix-IRR's Managing Partner and originating founder. He is an internationally recognised specialist in transformational change, strategy and sourcing, with over 20 years of experience in these fields. He was recently a Managing Partner in Accenture responsible for working with boards to shape their global transformational agendas.

GRAHAM BUSBY is a Partner, experienced in large, complex transformations. He works with Elix-IRR's most important clients helping them design target operating models for their support functions. Graham has experience advising multinational companies across a variety of industries, including retail, FMCG, transportation and media.

BARRI MAGGOTT is a Partner who leads Elix-IRR's African practice. Prior to Elix-IRR he was a Partner with KPMG. During his consulting career he was engaged with a wide range of clients mainly in the retail, financial services, and oil and gas industries. He has consulted on a number of business change programmes, encompassing the areas of IT, risk and finance, and has a deep understanding of business strategy and related operating models.

4. OUTSOURCING IN RETAIL

JOHN HAWKINS is a Partner specializing in large and complex change and outsourcing transactions, transforming multiple processes across various continents in highly competitive markets. John has worked with some of the largest European and US retailers on major transformation and sourcing programmes.

ADAM JOHNSON is a Partner with over 30 years' experience of consulting, sales and management, in technology and outsourcing, working with clients in most industries and in over 20 countries worldwide to develop and transform their businesses. Adam was one of the first Business Process Outsourcing (BPO) sales leaders, and has created pioneering relationships with, among others, Thames Water, BP, Volvo and Schlumberger.

ANTHONY POTTER is a Partner with deep consulting experience in sourcing and outsourcing strategy. His expertise is in shaping cost reduction strategies driven through effective procurement, outsourcing/offshoring strategy and process optimization. Prior to Elix-IRR, Anthony was at McKinsey and previously in Accenture's strategy team, working with clients in the retail and financial services industries.

FIGURES

FIGURE 1: Growth in Mobile Internet Users in the UK		11
FIGURE 2: Drivers of Retail Change		12
FIGURE 3: E-commerce Development Timeline		16
FIGURE 4: Examples of Digital Retailing in Action		17
FIGURE 5: How Retailers Can Stay Ahead		18
FIGURE 6: Example Applications of Digital's New Value Exchange		24
FIGURE 7: How Digital is Eroding Barriers to Entry		27
FIGURE 8: Conclusions		32
FIGURE 9: Global Handset Data Traffic 2001-2017		36
FIGURE 10: Kickstarter Digital Platform Case Study		37
FIGURE 11: General Electric Digital Platform Case Study		39
FIGURE 12: 7-Eleven Japan Digital Platform Case Study		40
FIGURE 13: Planning a Digital Platform		42
FIGURE 14: Non-cash Transactions 2001-2010 ($ billions)		45
FIGURE 15: Path of Innovation in Payments		46
FIGURE 16: Disruptive and Innovative Payment Companies		47
FIGURE 17: Examples of Today's Enterprises Using Innovative Payment Mechanisms		48
FIGURE 18: Capitalizing on Payments Innovation – Key Questions to Ask		49
FIGURE 19: Returns Rates Vary by Product Category		56
FIGURE 20: Integrated Planning: What Businesses Say		62
FIGURE 21: Overview of Additional Capabilities/Services That Can Be Delivered by a Central Office Function		63
FIGURE 22: Outputs of Integrated Business Planning		65
FIGURE 23: The Big Data Vicious Cycle		67
FIGURE 24: Examples of Use of Big Data		70
FIGURE 25: Big Data Capability Assessment Tool for Mainstream Retailers		72
FIGURE 26: Online Sales Forecast as a Percentage of Total Sales		72
FIGURE 27: Share of Sales Made Online in 2012		73
FIGURE 28: Important External Trends Driving the Need for Business Transformation over the Past Three Years		77

FIGURE 29: Stages of a Business Transformation Project with Highest Risk of Failure 78

FIGURE 30: With Which Element of the Change Management Initiative Has Your Organisation Had the Most Difficulty? 79

FIGURE 31: For Change Management Initiatives that Worked for Your Organisation in the Past 12 Months, What Was the Single Most Important Factor in Determining Success? 81

FIGURE 32: Key Questions to Ask During the Project Lifecycle 82

FIGURE 33: Transformation Lifecycle 82

FIGURE 34: Service Management Framework Building Blocks 85

FIGURE 35: Overview of the Key Building Blocks of the Service Management Framework 86

FIGURE 36: Organisational Excellence through Service Management 90

FIGURE 37: Elix-IRR's TOM Methodology 92

FIGURE 38: TOM Design Steps 92

FIGURE 39: 3 Core Tenets of TOM Design 94

FIGURE 40: The Five Steps to Ensuring Outsourcing Success 99

FIGURE 41: Example TOM for Facilities Management, Grouping the Location of Functions 104

FIGURE 42: Five Aspects of a Successful Outsourcing Deal 112

FIGURE 43: Recent Examples of Companies Developing Nearshore Operations 115

FIGURE 44: Potential Benefits of Nearshoring 117

FIGURE 45: Potential Cumulative Impact of Factors on Staff Cost Arbitrage (US & UK vs. Offshore Locations) 119

FIGURE 46: 2011 Office Space Prime Rents for Sample Offshore and Nearshore Locations (USD/sqft./month) 121

FIGURE 47: Forecast for Rental Price Movement, 2012 Onwards 121

FIGURE 48: Transition and Ongoing Management Costs as a Percentage of Total Offshoring Deal Value 123

FIGURE 49: Value of Global ITO/BPO Deals by Sector, 2011–12 125

FIGURE 50: Scope of IT Sourcing Deals in Retail 127

FIGURE 51: ITO Sub-Domain Outsourcing Activity, 2011 Total Contract Value (TCV) ($m) 128

FIGURE 52: Impact of Major Retail Trends on Technology and IT Sourcing 129

FIGURE 53: Overview of Elix-IRR's Collaborative Solutioning Methodology 136

FIGURE 54: Comparison of RFP and Collaborative Solutioning 138

BIBLIOGRAPHY

Arthur, L. (2013, July 26). *Five Ways Digital Disruption Will Impact The Customer Experience*. From www.forbes.com: http://www.forbes.com/sites/lisaarthur/2013/03/19/five-ways-digital-disruption-will-impact-the-customer-experience

Balaban, D. (2011, May 19). *Major New Bank Joins UK Contactless and NFC Landscape*. From NFC Times: http://nfctimes.com/news/major-new-bank-joins-uk-contactless-and-nfc-landscape

Batten, N. (2012, September 13). *Burberry Regent Street pilots interactive technology*. From http://www.marketingmagazine.co.uk/: http://www.marketingmagazine.co.uk/article/1149851/burberry-regent-street-pilots-interactive-technology

Buter, S. (2013, February 21). *John Lewis to extend online shopping empire via thousands of corner stores*. From http://www.theguardian.com/: http://www.theguardian.com/business/2013/feb/21/john-lewis-online-shopping-collect

Cabinet Office. (2011, July). *Government ICT Offshoring (International Sourcing) Guidance*. From Gov.uk: https://www.gov.uk/government/uploads/system/uploads/attachment_data/file/61159/government-ict-offshoring.pdf

Capgemini Consulting. (2012). *Trends in Business Transformation*. Capgemini Consulting.

Capgemini. (2012). *World Payments Report 2012*. From Capgemini Corporate Website: http://www.capgemini.com/sites/default/files/resource/pdf/The_8th_Annual_World_Payments_Report_2012.pdf

Clark, S. (2012, February 16). *Turkcell equips 300,000 customers with T-series NFC capable phones*. From http://www.nfcworld.com/2012/02/16/313298/turkcell-signs-up-300000-customers-for-nfc-mobile-wallet/

ComputerWeekly. (2005, October 27). *Sainsbury's scraps outsourcing deal with Accenture*. From http://www.computerweekly.com/: http://www.computerweekly.com/news/2240075660/Sainsburys-scraps-outsourcing-deal-with-Accenture

Cooper, R. (2009, August 24). *BT shuts graduate scheme: how companies are cutting costs without redundancies*. From The Telegraph: http://www.telegraph.co.uk/finance/recession/6079615/BT-shuts-graduate-scheme-how-companies-are-cutting-costs-without-redundancies.html

Costello, S. (2013, July 26). *How Many Apps are in the iPhone App*

Store? From ipod.about.com: http://ipod.about.com/od/iphonesoftwareterms/qt/apps-in-app-store.htm

Cushman & Wakefield. (2012, February). *Office Space Around the World, February 2012.* From Cushman & Wakefield Corporate Web site: http://www.cushmanwakefield.com/en/research-and-insight/2012/office-space-around-the-world-february-2012/

Douthit, D. (2012, January 30). *Solving The Product Return Problem In Consumer Gizmos.* From www.forbes.com: http://www.forbes.com/sites/ciocentral/2012/01/30/solving-the-product-return-problem-in-consumer-gizmos/

Economist Intelligence Unit. (2008). *A Change for the Better: Steps for Successful Business Transformation.* Economist Intelligence Unit.

Economist. (2013, August 12). *Out of the box.* From The Economist: http://www.economist.com/blogs/schumpeter/2013/08/3d-printing

Economist. (2012, May 3). *Return to vendor: a dress on loan.* From www.economist.com: http://www.economist.com/node/21548928

Econsultancy. (2013). Retrieved May 2013 from econsultancy.com

First National Bank. (2013). *eWallet.* From https://www.fnb.co.za/ways-to-bank/ewallet.html

Flacy, M. (2011, December 5). *Starbucks Mobile Apps Account for 26 million Transactions Over 2011.* From Digital Trends: http://www.digitaltrends.com/mobile/starbucks-mobile-apps-account-for-26-million-transactions-over-2011/

Flinders, K. (2011, November 21). *Francis Maude is unashamedly obsessed with procurement but what's in it for suppliers?* From Computerweekly.com: http://www.computerweekly.com/blogs/outsourcing/2011/11/francis-maude-is-unashamedly-obsessed-with-procurement-but-whats-in-it-for-suppliers.html

Flinders, K. (2011, October 9). *Study reveals sectors boosting investment in IT outsourcing.* From Computerweekly.com: http://www.computerweekly.com/news/2240106550/Study-reveals-sectors-boosting-investment-in-IT-outsourcing

GalaxE Solutions. (2012, May). From GalaxE Solutions, Inc. Web site: http://www.galaxesolutions.com/

General Electric Company. (2013, July 23). *Our Company.* From General Electric UK Web site: http://www.ge.com/uk/company/index.html

Goldfingle, G. (2013, January 2). *A quarter of UK shoppers use stores as showroom before price-checking online.* From Retail Week Web site: http://www.retail-week.com/multichannel/a-quarter-of-uk-shoppers-use-stores-as-showroom/5044342.article

Guglielmo, C. (2012, March 4). *Apple May Be World's First Trillion Dollar Company*. From http://www.forbes.com/: http://www.forbes.com/sites/connieguglielmo/2012/04/03/apple-may-be-worlds-first-trillion-dollar-company/

Gulati, R., Nohria, N., & Wohlgezogen, F. (2010, March). *Roaring Out of Recession*. From Harvard Business Review: http://hbr.org/2010/03/roaring-out-of-recession/ar/

IBM. (2012). *IBM Big Data Success Stories*. IBM.

ICICI Bank. (2013, September). *ICICI Bank launches 'Pockets by ICICI Bank'*. From http://www.icicibank.com/aboutus/article/icicibank-launches-pockets-by-icicibank.html

IDC Retail Insights. (2012, January). *Worldwide Retail Industry 2012: Top 10 Predictions*. From http://www.idc.com/getdoc.jsp?containerId=GRI232576

Information Services Group. (2012). *The TPI Index: Global Sourcing Market Data and Insights, Fourth Quarter and Full Year 2011*. Information Services Group.

Invest Northern Ireland. (2013, October 22). *Smart Support*. From www.investni.com: http://www.investni.com/index/locate/smart_support.htm

iZettle. (2013). *Start Taking Card Payments Today*. From www.izettle.com

John Lewis. (2013). *Our Website and App*. From www.johnlewis.com: http://www.johnlewis.com/inspiration-and-advice/john-lewis-mobile-website-and-app

Jones Lang LaSalle. (2012). *Asia Pacific Property Digest Fourth Quarter 2011: Record Take-up in 2011*. From Jones Lang LaSalle Corporate Web site: http://www.ap.joneslanglasalle.com/ResearchLevel1/research-onpoint-appd-2011-q4-asiapacific.pdf

Jones Lang LaSalle. (2012). *Tri-City Market Profile, Q4 2011*. Jones Lang LaSalle.

Jones Lang LaSalle. (2012). *UK Office Market Outlook, Q4 2011*. From Jones Lang LaSalle Corporate Web site: http://www.joneslanglasalle.co.uk/ResearchLevel1/UK%20Office%20Market%20Outlook%20Q4%202011.pdf

Jones Lang LaSalle. (2012). *United States Office Outlook, Q4 2011*. From Jones Lang LaSalle Corporate Web site: http://www.joneslanglasalle.co.uk/Pages/ResearchDetails.aspx?ItemID=7642

Jones Lang LaSalle. (2012). *Warsaw Office Market Profile Q4 2011*. From Jones Lang LaSalle Corporate Web site: http://www.bpcc.org.pl/att/ae9c0d5f-8ee4-43cd-a52b-873a32f2f598_office_market_profile_poland_q4-2011_eng.pdf

Jopson, B. (2013, July 29). *New stamping ground for Nike and Adidas*

BIBLIOGRAPHY <149

as 3D shoes kick off. From www.ft.com: http://www.ft.com/cms/s/0/1d09a66e-d097-11e2-a050-00144feab7de.html#axzz2aQ5KIYNZ

Kickstarter, Inc. (2013, July 23). *"What is Kickstarter?"*. From Kickstarter, Inc. Web site: www.kickstarter.com/hello?ref=nav

Kong, K. (2012, February 17). *'Hana N Wallet' - Virtual wallet? But Real!* From http://www.bankingandpaymentsasia.com/news/hana-n-wallet-virtual-wallet-but-real

KPMG. (2012, July 26). *Global IT-BPO Outsourcing Deals Analysis: April through June 2012.* From KPMG Web site: http://www.kpmginstitutes.com/shared-services-outsourcing-institute/insights/2012/2Q12-sourcing-advisory-global-pulse-report.aspx

Laney, D. (2001). *3D Data Management: Controlling Data Volume, Velocity, and Variety.* META Group.

Lunden, I. (2013, July 30). *Mobile Data Traffic To Grow 300% Globally By 2017 Led By Video, Web Use.* From www.techcrunch.com: http://techcrunch.com/2013/07/03/mobile-data-use-to-grow-300-globally-by-2017-led-by-video-web-traffic-says-strategy-analytics/,

Martec International. (2011, July). *IT in Retail 2011-2012.* From Research and Markets Web site: http://www.researchandmarkets.com/research/e7fb67/it_in_retail_2011

McCarty, D., & Jinks, B. (2012, January 19). *Kodak Files for Bankruptcy as Digital Era Spells End to Film.* From http://www.bloomberg.com/: http://www.bloomberg.com/news/2012-01-19/kodak-photography-pioneer-files-for-bankruptcy-protection-1-.html

McConnell, M., & Vidal, R. (2007). *The True Cost of Attrition.* From InContact, Inc. Corporate Web site: http://www.incontact.com/media/files/white-paper-attrition.pdf

McGulloch, S. (2012, October 12). *Clear Returns shortlisted in New York technology competition.* From http://www.business7.co.uk/: http://www.business7.co.uk/business-news/scottish-business-news/2012/10/12/clear-returns-named-as-only-non-us-finalist-in-new-york-technology-competition-106408-23932431/

McRae, H. (2013, January 20). It's pointless to focus on retailers' woe. *The Independent* , pp. http://www.independent.co.uk/news/business/comment/hamish-mcrae/hamish-mcrae-its-pointless-to-focus-on-retailers-woe-8458531.html.

Millar, M. (2013, January 28). *Return to sender: Why the Christmas boom can be a retail headache.* From http://www.bbc.co.uk/: http://www.bbc.co.uk/news/business-21148508

Morrell, L. (2013, February 19). *Analysis: The value of returns - what does it mean for your business?* From www.retail-week.com: http://www.

retail-week.com/in-business/supply-chain/analysis-the-value-of-returns-what-does-it-mean-for-your-business/5045410.article

OFCOM.

Overby, S. (2013, August 9). *Anti-Offshoring Bill Unlikely to Impact Call Center Industry*. From http://www.cio.com/: http://www.cio.com/article/737852/Anti_Offshoring_Bill_Unlikely_to_Impact_Call_Center_Industry

Overby, S. (2005, September 1). *Backsourcing Pain*. From CIO Magazine: http://www.cio.com/article/10524/Outsourcing_and_Backsourcing_at_JPMorgan_Chase

Overby, S. (2003, September 1). *The Hidden Costs of Offshore Outsourcing*. From CIO Magazine: http://www.cio.com/article/29654/The_Hidden_Costs_of_Offshore_Outsourcing

Palmer, M. (2012, August 15). *Large US retailers to create mobile wallet*. From Financial Times Web site: http://www.ft.com

Seven-Eleven Japan Co., Ltd. (2013, July 23). *Company Corporate Information*. From Seven-Eleven Japan Web site: http://www.sej.co.jp/company/en/s.growth.html

Spence, A. (2011, May 3). *Outsourcing industry 'is almost as big as finance'*. From The Times: http://www.thetimes.co.uk/tto/business/industries/supportservices/article3005674.ece

Square, Inc. (2013). *Anyone Can Accept Credit Cards with Square*. From Square Up: https://squareup.com/register

Strickland, N. (2000). PACS (picture archiving and communication systems): filmless radiology. *Arch Dis Child*, 82-86.

The Boston Consulting Group. (2012). *The Connected World: The Internet Economy in the G20*. The Boston Consulting Group.

The Economist. (2011, July 30). *The trouble with outsourcing*. From The Economist: http://www.economist.com/node/21524822

Ven. (2013). *About Ven*. From www.vencurrency.com/about

Ventana Research. (2010). *Integrated Business Planning: Redesigning Planning for a More Dynamic Business Environment*. Pleasanton, California: Ventana Research.

Virgin Atlantic. (2013). *The Virgin Experience: Upper Class*. From Virgin Atlantic Corporate Web site: http://www.virgin-atlantic.com/gb/en/the-virgin-experience/upperclass.html

Wallop, H. (2010, January 14). *John Lewis 'best shop in Britain'*. From http://www.telegraph.co.uk/: http://www.telegraph.co.uk/finance/newsbysector/retailandconsumer/6982124/John-Lewis-best-shop-in-Britain.html

Waters, R. (2013, June 19). *Inside Business: GE plans platform path for 'internet of things*. From FT.com.

We Use Coins. (2013). *Your Portal Into the World of Bitcoin*. From www.weusecoins.com/en/

Weill, P., & Ross, J. W. (2009). *IT Savvy*. Harvard Business Press.

Williams, J. (2011, June 13). *Tesco Launches Groceries Android App with Voice Searching Feature*. From Comupter Weekly: http://www.johnlewis.com/inspiration-and-advice/john-lewis-mobile-website-and-app

Withers, P. (2013, September 05). *Virgin Media to open new flagship store in Birmingham*. From Mobile News: http://www.mobilenewscwp.co.uk/2013/09/05/virgin-media-to-open-new-flagship-store-in-birmingham/